I Climbed A Mountain

A Mother's Diary of Tragedy, Grief & Triumph

by Kathi Pollard

Illustration by Julee Nordin

Copyright © 1996
Kathi Pollard

All rights reserved. No part of this book may be reproduced in any form, except for the inclusion of brief quotations in a review, without permission in writing from the author.

Printed in the USA
Morris Publishing
Kearney, Nebraska

First Edition
First Printing • 1996

ISBN 1-57502-409-8

Front cover designed courtesy of:
Julee Nordin
N13006 K-1 Rd.
Carney, MI 49881

Back cover photo by Kathleen Harpt, Marinette, WI.

To arrange speaking engagements, contact:
Kathi Pollard
P.O. Box 105
Stephenson, MI 49887

To purchase additional copies of this book, an order form at the back of this book is included for your convenience.

PREFACE

Grieving the loss of a child is akin to climbing a mountain, both literally and figuratively speaking. The journey is not so demanding at first; the overwhelming size of the mountain leaves you in a kind of stupor or shock, and so the first few precipices, though they may be difficult, are not genuinely felt on too deep a level. But as you scale the higher peaks ahead, the shock gradually wears off and harsh reality begins to set in.

Every step forward becomes more demanding and more torturous than the one before and, at some point, not only do you become supremely aware of the possibility of falling and plunging to your own death, but you begin to question your ability to press forward in such pain. Press forward, however, you must, for intuitively you know that you come down a mountain differently than you go up it, and in order to complete the journey and achieve the "coming down from" you must first get to the top.

The most curious aspect of mountain climbing is, however, that once you have achieved the summit and look across the boundless landscape before you, a new realization dawns true and sometimes foreboding - that the summit upon which you stand is only the beginning of more peaks yet to be conquered which are perhaps not as high or as challenging, but certainly as noble and as necessary a pursuit as the peak you have just scaled.

There is a grace that comes, I have discovered, as you are faithful in the pursuit of a new height, and God's breath is adequate for survival when the air seems to get too thin to breathe on your own. I encourage you to breathe deeply from His Spirit when the going gets particularly tough.

Although it often felt so, I now realize that I was never climbing alone, but that I was, in fact, roped to a Mighty God to whose faithfulness I am a living testimony. It was His almighty hand which supported me, His holy presence which sustained me, and His awesome grace which led me to higher ground.

To that end, and because of that realization, I offer this book to all those who are scaling their own mountains, be they small or huge. I encourage you to press forward, undaunted by the aches, pains and bruises you have already endured. The journey itself will have its own reward and, if I am correct, will prove to make you a stronger climber for the inevitable "next mountain" just over the ridge.

> "Though I walk through the valley
> of the shadow of death....
> Thou art with me."

DEDICATION

I lovingly dedicate this book
to my son and daughter-in-law,
Nathan and Jenny (Pomeroy) Pollard,
whose deaths catapulted my soul
into the deep, dark abyss known as grief;

and to my daughters,
Rachel and Sarah, whose lives
stir my faith and courage
to move forward with my life,
and who inspire me to continue
to love and to be loved.

ACKNOWLEDGEMENTS

First and foremost, I extend heartfelt gratitude to God for His patience with and faithfulness to me, especially during those times when I consciously chose to exclude Him from my life and my pain in grieving. He had shown Himself to be more loving and compassionate than ever I had imagined or believed Him to be.

I attribute a large portion of my spiritual, mental and physical well-being during the first year to those faithful and loving people I call my brothers and sisters in the Lord, especially to my pastor and those of the Stephenson Assembly of God Church. I pray that they never underestimate the power of love, prayer, compassion, letters, pot-roast dinners and spontaneous phone calls in contributing to the continuing recovery from trauma and heartache. I feel certain that my ongoing process of healing is very much related to my connectedness to such incredible and devoted people.

I am deeply indebted to my own dear family - Mike, Rachel and Sarah - for their unswerving love through both the good and the bad of our lives together, and for the unequivocable tolerance they displayed as I spent hour after hour in front of my computer screen in order to complete this project. They gave me the space I needed to work and the comfort zone required to recoup after a long day.

I am humbled when I think of the Pomeroy family, and Al and Judy in particular, who in spite of their own pain in losing Jenny stood with us in ours. We have remained "family" to each other though the tie that bound us is gone. They have brought to me beauty and new meaning to the word "in-laws."

To every extended family member and friend who left an imprint of care and concern on my soul during the "dark days," especially my brother Mike who called regularly "just to chat," I extend my deepest appreciation and gratitude.

To all who prayed for this project and to those who were the consummate cheerleaders with an abundant supply of encouragement and positive thought, I say "Bless you."

FOREWORD

In writing this book, my sole intention was not to offer any kind of psychological analysis of the grief work which is necessary in order to survive losing a child, but rather to as simply and honestly as possible present a picture of the grief which accompanies the loss of a child and the kind of journey upon which one's soul must embark in order to rediscover one's self as a result of such a trauma.

When I speak of the trauma of losing a child, it is in no way intended to diminish or minimize the terrible heartache which accompanies the loss of any one person who is loved and cherished by another. But, having lost a parent, parent-in-law, and two siblings, I must confess that none of those experiences, as hurtful as each was, debilitated me to the extent and for the duration that losing my son has. Grieving the loss of a child is a singularly unique experience for which there is no comparison. Losing a child violates all that we understand as normal, natural, acceptable and expected. For those reasons alone, losing a child complicates the whole of the grieving process.

There are any number of good books on the market today which will address the various aspects of grief such as its stages, grief work, therapy techniques, and so on. This is not intended to be that kind of book. Rather, it is my hope that grieving parents will pick up this book somewhere along their own grief road and find in it the solace of knowing that there are, indeed, universal aspects of grief and that what they may be experiencing at whatever stage they are at is not atypical.

Additionally, almost all those of us who travel through the grieving process ask ourselves at some juncture if, in fact, we are not losing our minds, or has someone else had these feelings as well. May this book put to rest those terrible fears that haunt grieving parents - the agony of thought that no one could possibly understand what this kind of grief feels like. It is a tragic but true fact that none of us was the first grieving parent, nor will we be the last. We are not alone on this bereavement journey.

While none of us can know precisely what it is that another is feeling, it is only a grieving parent who can have at least a "clue" as to what another grieving parent is experiencing. It is my hope that this book will help the friends of grieving parents have just a bit more of a sense of this kind of anguish so that they, in turn, can offer appropriate forms of love and support through the first year or two of the grieving process especially. Ultimately, each parent will work through each of the stages of grief at his/her own pace, and with his/her own style, but loving and supportive friends can be a Godsend and a gift to the parent in need of nurture and healing.

Finally, I must confess that my intentions in writing this book were not altogether altruistic for, in fact, the exercise of verbal/written expression is and continues to be one of the more therapeutic forms of grief work for me. But knowledge, in order to have any power and impact, must be shared so I pray that what I have learned and subsequently shared in this book will prove to be a source of guidance for others who are traveling the road known as grief. May God give us all grace, wisdom and strength for the journey.

I CLIMBED A MOUNTAIN

There's nothing quite like the Indian Summers of Northeastern Wisconsin, and Oct. 12, 1994, was no exception. It was an incredibly rare, almost exquisitely beautiful Wednesday. The breeze was warm and moist off the Bay of Lake Michigan. The oak and maple leaves seemed to arrogantly defy Mother Nature and clung tenaciously to the branches flashing their brilliant hues of gold and red. The temperature was unusually high, a record 73 degrees.

I was taking a couple of classes at the University Center in Marinette and tutoring English there on a part-time basis. My son Nathan and his wife Jenny, still in the newly-wed stage of marriage, were full-time students on the same campus. He was a sophomore and she a freshman. I had made a point of reminding myself that while on campus I was not Mom, but just another student. They, however, seemed less concerned about such issues than I and very often would wave to me from across the commons area or as they were on their way to classes, always with "Hi, Mom!" Occasionally, we'd have lunch in the cafeteria together, or we'd sit outside on a bench and just "catch up." Talk about blessing a mother's heart!

My office, located in the Library building, was next to the English classroom in which Jenny was taking a Comp I class so, more times than not, Nathan would lean against the wall just outside Jen's classroom door waiting for her to finish. The two would then stop by my office to say good-bye for the day. Sometimes they would just press their faces against the glass in my door and leave smile and kiss prints on it.

But on Oct. 12, things would be different. I got to classes late that morning, so I missed saying hello. They went home for lunch that day, so I did not see them in the cafeteria. We all were rushing to class after lunch, so a wave was all that got exchanged.

Because tomorrow was Nathan's birthday and I wanted to get home to wrap his present and start supper, I decided not to tutor that afternoon. Oh, I would miss not seeing their goofy grins and hearing their chatter down the hallway, but after all, I would see them both tomorrow when I took them out to lunch to celebrate Nathan's 20th birthday.

But tomorrow never came.

* * *

I left my office about 10 minutes before Jen's class would have dismissed. As I walked to the lot where I was parked, I saw their motorcycle, both helmets dangling from the handlebars, and had one of those silly thoughts.

"I should sit here on their bike wearing one of their helmets, and when they come out I should say something totally jerky like, "Hey, man, how 'bout a lift home?" knowing full well they'd be in a rush to get home and change since they were planning to go to Green Bay to attend a Christian Concert by White Cross. So I didn't do it.

Or maybe I should just hang around long enough to tell them to have a wonderful time tonight and not to be late for lunch tomorrow. But I didn't do it.

Instead, I walked to my car, jumped in and mentally planned my supper menu, all the while fighting off this nagging thought that I should go back and see the kids. The drive home takes nearly 30 minutes, and about 29 of those I spent feeling like something wasn't right. I should have stayed. I should have talked to them for a minute. I should have listened to my sixth sense. But I didn't.

* * *

I had been home for little more than an hour and had already wrapped Nathan's birthday present which he had picked out himself. Since his new status as a married man, he had become a bit more conscientious about his attire. He lived in jeans for the most part, but with three distinct categories: his one "awesome" pair, which he wore to church; his couple of "pretty cool" pair which he wore to school and around; and his "grubs" which he wore to his job at a food distributing warehouse. Now he wanted dress clothes and had picked out a new shirt, v-neck sweater and trousers. I picked up the tab, thrilled to accommodate. Packages successfully wrapped, I started on the spaghetti sauce.

As I was adding a pinch more oregano, a most peculiar sensation came over me. My heart began to race and my chest felt like it was in a vice grip. I could barely catch my breath and panic set in, completely out of the blue. My God, was I having a heart attack? I went to lie down on the couch, but my feet wouldn't move and so I slithered to a sitting position right there on the kitchen floor at the base of the stove.

It felt like an eternity before this phenomenon passed, but it did. I had no sooner stood up, intending to trying my hand at the spaghetti sauce again, when Mike's truck pulled into our drive. He was a half-hour early, but it didn't seem at all odd since occasionally he goes in to work early and then comes home a bit early.

He came into the kitchen and just stared at me for a moment with an ashen face. Somehow I knew. I listened to the words he said, but somehow I knew even before he said them.

"I've just gotten the worst news in the world."

I wanted to say, "What?" but it wouldn't come out.

"Nathan and Jen were on their way home from school. There was an accident....a truck....they were both killed."

I collapsed to the floor again. This time my heart was not racing, my breath was not labored. Instead, an invisible force had reached down into the warm crevice between my breastbone and ripped my beating heart from where it had nestled and placed it, cold, dead, heavy, and stonelike right in the middle of my throat.

I wanted to scream; I wanted to cry out like a wounded, trapped animal, but nothing would come out. I just sat there. By now Mike was on the floor next to me, trying to hold me, but I don't remember feeling any sensation of touch, or smell, or sound. I had fallen into an abyss so deep, dark and torturous that absolutely nothing was registering, with one exception. My stomach erupted and I retched what seemed to be everything I had ever put into it for the last 42 years.

* * *

It is a wonder to me, retrospectively, how instinctual we humans can be. To this day, I don't remember any details of the next 12 hours. We made phone calls to family, pastor, and friends; people came in and out with food, hugs and tears; the State Police came by to inform us of the necessity of autopsies and I vaguely remember being offended that they wanted to "cut" my children; everyone kept insisting that I eat, or that I rest, or that I take "something," but it remains mostly fog in my memory. My first distinct memory is of the following day's trip down to the funeral home to make arrangements for the wake and burial which would be held Friday night and Saturday morning.

I would come to discover what blessed buffers shock and denial can be in traumatic situations. My first revelation of this was during a conversation with Mike on the way to the funeral home Thursday morning.

Nathan had been growing a beard for hunting season; it wasn't really full yet, just at that scraggly stage. I had always thought he was far more handsome without it and had begun the conversation to that end.

"Mike, remind me to tell Gary (our friend and funeral director) to be sure to shave Nathan's face. I don't want him to have that scraggly growth."

Dead silence.

"Mike? Let's make sure Gary shaves Nate's face, okay?"

"Kath, that won't be...you don't need to...it's not really an issue."

I don't know if at that point I really didn't understand what he was trying to tell me, or if I needed to hear him say aloud that which I certainly didn't want to hear.

"What do you mean?"

"Nathan's injuries were mostly to the head...his head was....it was bad, Kath. I doubt if they'll even be able to show him."

Somehow I knew it....a motorcycle, a truck, death on impact, but my mind could not fully comprehend the full extent of that scenario and it would be months later before I would actually begin to ask the appropriate hows and whys of those who had been at the scene of the accident. Right now all I could absorb with any clarity was that I would not see Nathan's face again, the face I had loved and kissed and teased and adored. It was too much and I sobbed uncontrollably for just a few moments. It was as if my body was on a timer; I was being allowed to "feel" for only fleeting moments and then this dull, controlled numbness would set back in, and I would attempt whatever task was at hand.

* * *

I have a deep respect and regard for funeral directors. I cannot imagine having parents come into my office after losing a child, or children, and being able to gently and lovingly walk them through the necessary steps of preparation for the wake and funeral.

Gary and Bev Anderson were there waiting for us in their office when we arrived. Jenny's parents, Judy and Al Pomeroy, arrived just after we did. I was a basket case; Mike was quiet and remote, although he displayed an incredible sense of "take charge" as we began the process of writing obits, picking out caskets, and so on. Al wept unabashedly for his little girl; Judy displayed the quiet, strong courage for which she is so well known. Gary and

Bev were simply "there," offering sincere and appropriate comments as necessary. As Christians themselves, and knowing we all shared a common faith, they could have easily wriggled out of this painful setting with a few well-placed platitudes about God and faith, but they didn't. They stood with us in our pain; comforted us as best they could; offered us love and support. I wouldn't come to appreciate their efforts until later when others equally as sincere but more uncomfortable with grieving parents would, in fact, say things that would only add to our pain rather than help to soothe it.

* * *

Gary told us that Nathan was "too badly injured" to be shown. At the time, I quietly acquiesced to his insistence that there be a closed casket for Nathan; Jenny would be shown for though her injuries were as extensive as Nathan's, they were less apparent and Gary felt an open casket for her would be an appropriate decision. Obituaries were written; caskets and burial vaults were chosen; appropriate sacred music would be furnished by an organist during the entirety of the wake; Jenny's siblings took it upon themselves, with our blessing and gratitude, to purchase the flowers for the caskets and as accents for around the room.

As we left the office, I turned around to look at the package I had brought in. Today would have been Nathan's 20th birthday and there, lying on the office desk, was his new outfit. Nathan would be buried in his birthday clothes and I wouldn't even get to see him in them.

* * *

I, who normally never function well without at least six hours of sleep per night, was now at the brink of total exhaustion, not having slept at all since receiving the news of their deaths. Finally, at 2 a.m. the day of the wake, I took a sedative and slept until 6:15. A nightmare about Nathan's dying woke me - and then I realized it was not a nightmare at all, but the harsh reality of my life prodding me out of a drug-induced stupor into immediate alertness and watchfulness. I got up and checked on both of the girls, each sleeping the sleep of denial. Mike heard me get up and tried to encourage me to come back to bed and to try to rest since we would have a very demanding day ahead, but I could not lie down.

I felt like a caged animal, pacing back and forth, waiting for someone to spring the gate of the trap in which I was confined. My heart pounded wildly as if I had been running a marathon. My stomach felt like it would explode at any moment. Every fiber of my being was twisted, contorted and knotted. I would have cried out to God but I was far too angry with Him to even acknowledge His existence. I have never known such pain or torture. And then it happened - at last - the sweet release of hot, bitter, angry tears. And I cried as I have never cried before; I sobbed uncontrollably; I lay on the kitchen floor in a fetal position and wept till it seemed there could be no tears left in me.

Suddenly, as before, a timer went off inside me and the tears immediately ceased. My heart had quieted down; my stomach didn't feel well enough to receive food, but the knots in it and the rest of my body had diminished. A thought, a desire, a need kept swirling around inside me and I went to the phone and called Gary.

"Gary, this is Kathi. I know you said we couldn't see Nathan, but I have to see him. I don't care what you do to his head, or how you do it, or if you want to cover him from the shoulders up; I don't care, but I have to see him. I have to touch him, Gary. I will not bury him until I can say goodbye," all punctuated with quiet sobbing.

There was a long, deliberate pause at the other end and finally,

"Well, Kathi, I think I can understand your need. I don't know what I can do, but I'll think of something. Okay,

Kath? We'll work out something, Kath. I don't know quite what, but we'll work out something."

The girls were awaking just as I hung up the phone. I showered. Rachel helped Sarah eat breakfast. Then we all just sat in the living room like prisoners awaiting their own executions - waiting, hoping, praying that there would be a last-minute reprieve from the inevitable event of getting into the car and driving to the funeral home. But the phone call from the "governor" never came; we made the "long walk" to Menominee in absolute silence. What had we done to deserve this punishment? Why won't someone rush up to us and tell us it's all been a terrible, horrible mistake, and that we are free to leave - that our loved ones will be waiting for us back home?

* * *

Judy and Al and their children were already there when we arrived. The heavy smell of flowers and freshly potted and misted plants hung in the air. I felt like I couldn't get any oxygen into my lungs; my knees kept wanting to buckle under me; the usual knot in my stomach was now a blade of steel, piercing my insides with every move my body attempted to make.

We all assembled into Gary's office. A few minor exchanges of conversation punctuated the heaviness and somberness in the room.

Gary explained to us that we would view Jenny first and then, for those who wanted to view Nathan, he would open his casket once we had paid our final respects to Jenny. The inevitable moment came; Gary led us into the room where the children lay in state.

Al and Judy, Mike and I went in first, followed by our children. There in the front of the room stood two caskets, one opened, one closed. I felt as if I were walking in slow motion - my legs wouldn't cooperate and just dragged behind me ever so slowly.

I had grown to love Jenny as my own. She was so much a part of our family that it seemed only natural to think of her as a Pollard even before the kids had married. And now I had to say goodbye to this once-vibrant 18-year-old woman-child whom I had been blessed to call my daughter-in-law.

Such odd thoughts kept surfacing as I gazed down upon her. Someone had fixed her hair just the way she liked best to wear it. The dress she was wearing, originally intended to be this year's Christmas present from her mom, was the perfect green for her eyes, now closed in death. Even a swollen face as a result of her injuries could not distract from her beauty. Her Bible lay next to her. I kept thinking that at any minute she would stretch, yawn and wake up, and then giggle her famous comes-right-from-her toes giggle. I finally walked away and sat down and stared at the setting itself.

Their caskets were set in a V-shape. At the tip of the V was their wedding picture set on a pedestal and surrounded by wreaths and cascades of red and pink roses. Nathan's casket, still closed, was topped with a large portrait of him, his Bible and a large spray of red roses matching the one on Jen's casket. The entire front of the room was filled with flowers and baskets of green plants and shrubs. Even as I sat there, dozens more were arriving. The room was beginning to look like a veritable greenhouse, and the air was getting thicker and stuffier by the moment.

I was vaguely aware that people were beginning to arrive, mostly extended family, but I couldn't make my body turn around to acknowledge them. I sat there, stone cold and stiff, staring at the closed casket in front of me.

Jenny's family lingered around her for quite some time; I caught snatches of the conversation, but none of it registered. Then Gary came from the back and asked if we'd like to see Nathan now. Judy was on one side of me, Mike on the other, as Gary lifted the lid. I remember my knees finally giving way and Judy's arm around my waist supporting me as I regathered myself. I'm not sure what I had been expecting to see, but I think I had convinced myself that it wouldn't be Nathan who would be revealed to me. My denial was shattered to a thousand pieces for there he lay dressed in his birthday outfit.

I checked every detail of his clothes as if he were going out on a date, or to an important event. I couldn't bear to look at his face, but I knew I must. His entire head, which was more oblong than round from the injuries sustained as a result of being trapped under the truck, was wrapped in white gauze with only a tuft of his blonde hair peaking out at the top. I cupped his cheek, wishing, longing, desperately needing to feel that scraggly growth I had wanted them to shave off. I stroked the small tuft of hair; how very blonde it looked against the satin pillow. I could sense people leaving from behind me - mostly Jenny's family, as I recall - but I stood there and just held his hand.

I loved Nathan's hands. They were so massive and could do remarkable things. I would always be astounded when he could come in from the driveway after hurling basketballs and slam-dunking, and would quietly sit at the piano and play an incredibly intricate piece of music with heartfelt finesse and delicacy. He would pick his little sister up with such strength and twirl her around till she giggled herself into exhaustion, and then would walk over to Jenny and gently cup her face with those same strong, massive hands.

And so, I just held his hand as I said goodbye. I had seen him. I had touched him. I turned to Gary and said, "You may close the casket now," and went to join Mike and the Pomeroys in the receiving line for what would be seven of the longest hours of my life.

* * *

We arrived home after the wake at approximately 11 p.m. We had been at the funeral home since 2 p.m. I had been unable to eat all day; I hadn't slept for two consecutive nights; I was exhausted beyond description. Everytime I tried to close my eyes that night all I could see were lines and lines of faces in front of me - people sobbing, people with blank stares, friends and family whose tortured countenances kept flashing before my eyelids. My body actually ached from leaning up, down, and across to people who wanted to hug, hold, be hugged or be held.

It was one of the largest and longest wakes in the history of the county and every fiber of my being confirmed it. I finally got up at midnight to take a sleeping pill and decided to take only one-half of one knowing that I would need to be up again early the following morning to prepare the girls and myself for the funeral. I did not want to be in any more of a stupor than I already was experiencing.

My body responded quickly to the meds; I don't remember even falling asleep. But at 3 a.m. my sleep was broken when I awoke with incredible chest pains that were moving up my chin and down my left shoulder. I could not breathe; a cold sweat had begun to break out upon my forehead.

I reached over and grabbed Mike's arm. He was awake instantly. I could barely talk for lack of air. Mike called our neighbor, an EMT on the local rescue squad team. She brought oxygen, took my blood pressure and pulse and insisted we call the ambulance.

The nearest hospital was 40 minutes away, so arrangements were made for a paramedic intercept en route. The paramedics administered an IV and nitroglycerine. By the time I had arrived at the hospital I had been stabilized. An EKG would show no specific sign of an actual heart attack. A young ER physician, who was told by the squad members of the trauma in our family, rather coldly announced to me that I could go home, it was "merely a panic attack." I wasn't sure whether to thank him, or hit him. He prescribed a tranquilizer and compazine for my retching stomach and released me only an hour before the funeral was to take place.

Mike, who had stayed behind at home so as not to leave the girls alone, had called my father who was spending the night in a motel only a few minutes from the hospital. He, along with my brother and sister-in-law, stayed with me till I was officially released. I sent Dad to the funeral; Tom and his wife Gina brought me home. I knew I simply could not attend the funeral without a repeat of what had just happened a few hours earlier.

I readily confess that, to this day, I am not sorry to have missed it. I had said my good-byes the night before. More importantly, I intuitively knew I did not have it in me to watch two caskets being lowered into a single, gaping hole in the earth. I could not bear the thought of burying my children. It was the inevitable conclusion to this whole thing called death, but I could not deal with it, not now, not yet.

Someday I would go to the grave. Someday I would touch the soil and sod which covered the bodies of my beloved children. But not now, not today.

I spent the rest of the day of the funeral sitting in the living room clad in my pajamas and robe. I didn't have the strength to shower or dress.

After the luncheon which followed the funeral service and burial, several of my friends came to the house to see me and express their concern. Each tried to find something to say or to do which she/he hoped would bring a measure of comfort, but I was still feeling the lingering effects of a sedative and very little was actually registering.

Eventually the house emptied of visitors. Mike and Rachel found places for the multitude of bowls, pans and dishes of food which had been brought in. I weaved my way through the thirty or forty plants that Gary and Bev had brought from the funeral home and went to bed. I slept sporadically till dawn. I awoke to realize it was Sunday.

* * *

I have always loved Sundays. It was the best day of the week in my estimation. It was the day I went to church, the day set aside to formally worship God with my family and my church family. It was our family day. Nathan and

Jen almost always came home on Sundays to be with family. When they would attend church with us, they'd come to dinner at our house and would then have supper with Jen's family. When they went to church with the Pomeroys, the procedure was reversed.

So when the phone rang that morning I instinctively thought, "Oh, good, Nathan's calling to see if they can come to dinner," and I ran to the phone with full anticipation of hearing his voice on the other end.

I don't recall who it was that actually called, or what the call was about. The only thing which registered with any clarity was the pain in realizing it was not Nathan's voice and never again would be. With that realization came my first taste of what would be many, many months of a deep, intense anger.

My list of those who were the object of my anger was not too exclusive. I was angry with myself. Why hadn't I stayed a bit longer at school that day? Maybe the entire afternoon's events would have been altered and the kids might still be alive as a result.

I was angry with Mike. Why hadn't he tried harder to talk Nathan out of getting the motorcycle in the first place? He knew how I hated the thought of Nathan and Jen cruising around on that thing! Why hadn't he simply demanded that they sell it?

I was angry with Nathan. Why did he love living on the "edge" as it were? Why did he consider life just one big adventure? Had he done everything he could to avoid the accident? Why had he taken the truck route home instead of First Street?

I was angry with Jen. Why did she have to go along with all of Nathan's crazy dreams and pursuits? Why didn't she put her foot down when it came to buying the bike? Why did she have to love it as much as he did?

But mostly, I was angry with God. How could He have let this happen? Why didn't He spare my children? Why did they have to die, much less in such a violent manner?

Kathi Pollard

How could He have betrayed the faith and confidence I had placed in Him to protect my kids? Why? Why? Why?

My life was replete with questions for which there seemed no answers. My anger continued to blaze, fueled by the seeming silence from heaven.

* * *

Only six days had passed since their deaths, but it already felt like an eternity. It was Oct. 18, the day before my forty-third birthday. Unlike many of my friends who were not happy about passing into their forty-something years, I always loved my birthdays.

I had brought Nathan home from the hospital on my twenty-third birthday. The doctor had never expected me to carry Nathan to full term and, indeed, he was five weeks early. I developed a number of medical complications throughout the pregnancy which only added to my doctor's concern for both Nathan's and my well being. I always believed that Nathan's birth and my quick recovery were both miracles, and told Nathan as much whenever an opportunity presented itself.

As he grew older, our birthdays began to take on more significance to him. Very often we would celebrate them together at his insistence. But he would not be here this year to take me to lunch. I would not be buying tickets to the symphony this October. My birthday would no longer celebrate the giving of life. Now it only would commemorate the remembrance of death.

* * *

My dear friend Terry called early the morning of my birthday. She was insistent that I get out of the house, even for a little while, and join her for lunch in Menominee. Try as I may, I could not convince her that I simply wanted to be alone, to forget that it was my birthday. After much cajoling, and a promise that I would not have to stay very long, I agreed to meet her at one of our favorite restaurants.

After we had ordered lunch, she handed me a package with a card atop it. In her wisdom she had chosen a blank card rather than a birthday greeting. In it she wrote of her love and concern for me and of her willingness to "be there" for as long as I needed her.

As I was opening the package, she explained its contents to me. It was a journal. As I thumbed through the pages, whiteness stared back at me.

"You've got to think about ways to express your pain, Kath. I thought maybe this could be one avenue for you. I know how you love to write. Maybe the words won't come right away, but if you start with just little thoughts, maybe it will help release some of the anguish you're experiencing."

I thanked her. I knew she loved me. I knew she wanted to help. I sensed her feeling of helplessness. But all I could think of for the entirety of the day was that there simply are no words to express this kind of heartache. Still, I had had enough psychology and counseling classes to know she was right.

That night, before trying to sleep, I made my first of what would be a year's worth of entries. Sometimes the thoughts came sporadically and haltingly; other times I couldn't write quickly enough to keep up with what was flowing through my heart and my head. But in every instance, I tried most of all to be honest with what I was experiencing. In retrospect, journaling proved to be one of the more effective forms of grief work for me.

Oct. 19, 1994

My life has been shattered into a million pieces, with no foreseeable hope of repair. I am so utterly devastated and hopelessly damaged - even if God were to try to fit all the fragments back together, I would and will forever be incomplete. Some of my pieces are lost to me forever; they are irretrievable and even God Himself cannot bring them back. I am forever changed, my composition forever altered, and now life requires of me a march through the regiment of living with a broken heart and a fractured soul. This is more than any mother should be demanded to do. I cannot.

Oct. 20, 1994

It is 5 a.m. Sleep is impossible. I close my eyes only to see the sweet faces of my Nathan and Jenny. In my mind I run to hug them and then I realize his face is gone and I hug and kiss only white bandages. I awake in tears, my body convulsing with sobs; I am soaking in perspiration; my heart's beat will not slow down or steady itself. I am tortured. This agony is more than I can bear. If it were not for my concern for Rachel and Sarah, I would ask God to release me from this through death itself.

Oct. 21, 1994

I have begged God repeatedly, through my tears, to allow Nathan to come to me for just a moment...to see his body restored and his beautiful face...to hear him tell me he is well and happy with his family in heaven...to give me some measure of comfort from this agony of separation. He has neither heard nor answered me. Perhaps He is not God at all.

It is 4:15 a.m. The nights are so very long. Even with a sedative, I sleep sporadically and restlessly. I long for daylight - the hope that there is a tomorrow - only to discover that tomorrows hold no promise, no healing, no respite. They are as empty and as torturous as the nights. Mike is in such pain, but my own is so overwhelming, I withdraw to my own personal hell and do not offer him comfort. I am sorry for that.

9:15 P.M.: We returned from Green Bay late this afternoon; I had a doctor's appointment with my cardiologist. He wanted to do an echogram. I thought to myself, "An EKG will be impossible - my heart has been ripped from me."

Dr. Fergus assures me that my valve has not been compromised or sustained any additional or permanent damage...it looks relatively healthy. He is right. I will not die from a bad heart - only a broken one.

Oct. 22, 1994

Settling Nathan's and Jen's estate is exhausting. The paperwork seems endless and tedious. Laywers and insurance adjustors want to be helpful and are trying to expeditiously settle things for us. I don't want to talk about money or double indemnities. I want what no one can give me - my son and daughter-in-law back again.

I was awakened this morning by a horrible nightmare. An invisible force propelled me into a line of people waiting to ride the roller coaster. I hate the roller coaster ride and try desperately to remove myself from the line of faceless people, but a force thrusts me forward and I am admitted through the gate into a black seat with no restraint or harness and no one else with whom to sit.

It is dusk and the ride begins. I can see the first dip and incline coming so I brace myself, but it is not as frightening as I had anticipated.

We approach a turn and an immediate drop. Suddenly my heart begins pounding more strongly. I want off this ride, but I look ahead and all I can see is miles and miles of track with no end in sight.

It is getting darker and the ride is getting more treacherous by the moment. Suddenly I am in blackness and I cannot see what's ahead. I feel the speed of the car. I am jutted from turn to turn, drop to incline. I cling desperately to the bar as my body is catapulted from side to side, back and forth, in my seat. I try to scream out for help, but I have no voice.

The ups and downs, backs and forths, are so extreme now that I can no longer hold on. I am confident that I will not survive the unknown, blackness, unanticipated. I decide to let go of the bar and be thrown from my seat to my death...and then I awake.

It was then I realized I am still alive. I put on my clothes. I washed my face. And then some mysterious force propelled me forward and a new realization is birthed -- I am again in the line heading for the roller coaster, only this time I am wide awake.

I remember when Nathan was about to be born - the incredible pain and wrenching of my body. The very flesh on my ribs, the muscle and sinew, all screamed in rebellion of the act of birth...and then I held him.

And now, 20 years later, Nathan has died and my insides are being wrenched and ripped again, and the whole of my body screams out in agony. Dear God, I would gladly endure this pain if only I could hold him again.

I have lost my son. Until now, the word "lost" held little sense of permanency. I've lost mittens, car keys and the like over the years. All were either found or easily replaced.

I have lost my son and I cannot find him. I search for his face in the window of my office. I listen for his voice in every incoming phone call. I reach for his arms' embrace after our family's Sunday dinners. He is truly lost to me and I am haunted by that awareness.

My stomach hurts all the time; my chest is heavy and my throat is constantly constricted to fight back the steady flow of tears. I cry over everything. I cry over nothing. I have lost a valuable treasure which will never be found and can never be replaced. There is an understanding deep within - I have lost my Nathan - I have lost me.

And where was God when we were being lost?

* * *

The University held an outdoor memorial service for Nathan and Jenny a week after the funeral. I was very touched that they had thought even to do such a thing and was especially moved to see how many of the students and professors attended it.

Nathan's basketball teammates had inscribed their names upon a basketball as a memorial. One of his best friends sang one of Nathan's favorite songs by Michael W. Smith entitled "Friends."

I Climbed A Mountain

I addressed his friends and professors on behalf of the Pomeroys and our family. I thanked them for loving our children, for contributing to the lives of Nathan and Jenny and for supporting us during this difficult time.

The ceremony was closed when Buffy, Nate's and Jen's good friend and schoolmate, released two bunches of balloons, one with 18 and the other with 19 - each balloon signifying the number of years Jenny and Nathan had spent on this earth. As the bright colors floated overhead in a brilliant blue sky and blew away to the north, I remember thinking that the balloons should have been black and the sky should have been cloudy and gray. It was far too beautiful a day to commemorate death. We should have been celebrating their lives.

I went back to school a week and a half after the funeral, not so much because I felt I needed to return and especially not because I wanted to get on with my life somehow, but basically because I simply didn't know what else to do with myself. I couldn't stand being at home. The house, in reality a small, modest ranch house, seemed like a huge, cold, mausoleum. I wandered around, from room to room, accomplishing absolutely nothing of purpose or substance. Often I would find myself quite literally just walking...walking from the bedroom to the living room, from the living room into the kitchen, then downstairs into Nathan's bedroom, and then immediately back upstairs to the bathroom...like a dazed child searching for her most valued little treasure which she has lost or misplaced.

I couldn't feel anything at all. I certainly didn't laugh, but I couldn't cry either; I felt no sense of happiness or joy, yet I could feel no semblance of pain or sadness. It was as if I was an empty shell, or a wound-up mechanical doll. I moved, I ate, I went to bed, I showered, I dressed, I washed dishes, I hugged daughters, I answered phones, I folded laundry; but it was all so hollow and meaningless. I convinced myself I needed to get back to school, back to routine, back to that which I had always loved - learning, back "into" life.

* * *

Oct. 23, 1994

Sundays are terrible. I tried to go to church. If I look to the right, I see Nathan playing the beautiful wedding song he wrote for Jenny and the incredible love that flowed between them that night in the candlelight.

If I look to the left, I see the spot in which Nathan and Jenny always chose to sit for worship. I see their faces turned upward, hands lifted in praise. I can still feel Jen's arms around me our last Sunday together as she prayed for me and whispered how very special I was to her. They were a delight to behold.

And if I look straight ahead, I see the cross. While I intellectually know that God also "lost" His only Son, I am in no position emotionally to accept it as a source of comfort. If He knew what pain I would endure, why didn't He prevent it? I have been faithful - where was He? Where were the angels? Where were the miracles?

I cannot stand Sundays right now. I cannot go to church right now. It is too soon, and I am too wounded.

Oct. 26, 1994

Terrible thoughts wash over me with no warning. I think of Nathan's last moments - how aware he must have been that he was about to be badly hurt - the panic he had to feel as he slid into the truck - his concern for his beloved Jen.

I cannot bear the thought of him suffering. It is torturous - it haunts me both on a conscious and unconscious level.

I am so angry with God. What did He possibly achieve through Nathan's and Jen's deaths that could not have been done through their lives? Where was He when they most needed Him? Did He at least keep them from suffering before the impact?

A thousand "whys" and only silence from heaven.

Oct. 30, 1994

Sundays are still the hardest to get through. It took all the courage I owned to go to church this morning. Worship was unbearable and impossible. I cannot praise God - I am far too angry with Him and hurt at His apparent failure toward my children and me. If Satan was trying to find a way to break my otherwise unshakeable faith, he has been successful.

I long for Nathan more than the air I breathe. I need to hear Jen chuckle at one of his silly jokes. I want him to come into my kitchen and pick me up off the floor with one of his hugs and listen to Jenny scold him for not being more tender. I want to see them at the dining table after church and listen to the adventures of their week together. I want us to be a whole family again. I need to feel the connection again. Maybe that is what prompted my visit to his grave this afternoon.

A part of me cannot accept that he is gone. I knelt by his grave and just wept hot bitter tears. He is gone and has taken everything that was good in me with him. I am empty. I am lost. I am forsaken. My anguish knows no bounds. I am damaged beyond repair. I shall never fully recover from this. I don't care whether or not I do. I am forcing myself to live, but every part of me wants to die.

Nov. 10, 1994

Occasionally the nights have been a refuge to me. I spend my days mechanically and obligatorily performing the required and mundane tasks of living, but in the blanket of blackness and the solitude of my room I can release the torturous pain I feel all day long.

There are those nights when I am inconsolable and I literally sob myself to a restless and brief sleep. Sometimes the ache is a dull, persistent pressure against my breast and tears stream quietly but steadily from my cheeks to my pillow.

On still other nights, my body lay motionlessly on its back while my mind furtively travels over twenty years of sights, sounds and sensations connected to Nathan. Then I etch from memory every single detail of his face on the ceiling above me - his golden-blonde hair always cut short and sporty - the tiny scar over his right eye from a stumble into the corner of a Tonka truck at 17 months old which is barely discernible through bushy eyebrows - the peculiar color of his eyes, not blue or green, but teal - the crooked smile with a chip out of his lower front tooth from a collision with an elbow while going up for a rebound under the hoop - his strong jaw and chiseled cheekbones - and I long for what will never be mine again in this lifetime.

Tonight, one month after their deaths, I have for the first time since the funeral prayed - a simple prayer. It was all I could find in me. "Please, God, make this pain go away. I can bear it no longer."

Certainly nothing profound, deep or theological, but it is, perhaps, a start - a return - a turning point. Dare I hope?

I asked Mike to make a simple wooden cross for the gravesite. I was there this week and a sudden panic set in when I realized how difficult it would be to "find them" after the first snowfall, since we will not be able to put a marker on their gravesite until spring. I somehow couldn't bear the thought that I would lose them over the winter. I do not understand my need for this connection to them. I know the grave is merely a resting place for their bodies - that their "essence" is in eternity, yet I have this almost irrational need to be there with them. I cannot let go. I long for something to which I can cling. Will this sense of desperation ever fade?

Nov. 12, 1994

It has been a full month. I planned my day carefully so as to be fully and completely occupied till bedtime, but I could not task at anything and, at one point this afternoon, became so inexplicably exhausted that I actually lay down on the couch and slept for an hour. I hate what is happening to my life - no control - no predictability - no security or sense of permanence and safety. I want to be done grieving, but I can't imagine ever <u>not</u> grieving the loss of my precious children. Dear God, will this never end?

Nov. 14, 1994

Driving back and forth to school is difficult emotionally. I'm left alone with my thoughts - isolated from any human touch or contact. It is at these times of the day that I seem to miss him the most.

Occasionally, something at school will set me off. Today, on the way to my Psych class, a young six-foot-or-so blonde-haired fellow came out of a class and crossed right in front of me. For just a moment I wanted to say, "Hey, Nathan! How's class going?" Then, of course, I realized it wasn't him. I fell apart right in the hallway and found myself racing for the closest bathroom.

I did get to class, and only a few seconds late, but I really wasn't there. Trouble is, I don't know where I was - if anywhere at all.

Nov. 16, 1994

It is 4:35 a.m. I got up at midnight and took one-half of a sleeping pill, but now I am wide awake again. My mind still plays "games" and occasionally I actually think that this is <u>all</u> a mistake - that the phone will ring and Nathan will be at the other end, his voice filled with the wry humor I had come to love.

I cannot turn my head off tonight. I want him home for Thanksgiving Dinner. I want Jenny to bring a jello mold and to help me with dishes afterward. There is no sequence to my thoughts...I want to put all of their wedding pictures into a photo album. I think about how I should put the boxes of Nathan's basketball trophies and track medals in the attic. The attic makes me think about his baby clothes and quilts which are stored up there until he has his own children. Children make me think of my grandchild, Angel, born stillborn. I only held her for a moment. She was so very tiny. Tiny makes me think about the weight I have lost and I get very frightened that my immune system has been damaged by stress and that my cancer will return as a result. What if I die of cancer and leave my girls motherless? Motherless makes me miss my own, dead less than a year. Is she holding her first great-grandchild right now?

I am so tired - so very, very tired.

***

Although each of us experiences and responds differently to grief, it is a universally accepted fact that the grieving process itself places very specific demands upon our bodies. Chronic fatigue often is part of the experience as is a nervousness due to biochemical changes within each of our systems.

I was not long into the grieving process when I could see a pattern emerging. I would have stretches of incredible fatigue and chronic exhaustion followed by unbelievable surges of energy and nervousness which demanded a release of some kind. The worst part of the experience was that the pattern was backward for me. The fatigue almost always occurred during the day; the spurts of perpetual motion, as I called them, occurred during late night to early morning.

It was not unusual to find me at 2:00 in the morning scrubbing the bathroom floor, scouring the tub, or cleaning the grout between the tiles for several months after the funeral. By December there wasn't a room, a floor, a closet or a drawer in my house that was not neatly organized and immaculately clean.

Because I started to become concerned about waking my children, I discovered other, more quiet, ways of dealing with the nervousness. I took up knitting with a fury and began to make cotton wash cloths. It wasn't long before I had such a collection of them that they actually took up a whole shelf in the linen closet. I called them my grief cloths, and gave them as birthday, anniversary, Christmas, and just-because-I-care gifts. Knitting became a quiet occupation in the early morning hours when I needed a physical outlet; my grief cloths proved to be a tangible expression of my pain. When I started giving them away, it was an opportunity to talk about what had provoked their construction and allowed me to share my grief with someone else. Eventually, I slept more at nights and knitted less, but having a physical project at those times of chemical imbalance served an important function in the road to maintaining both my health and my sanity.

Nov. 21, 1994

I went to church this morning and became emotionally shattered during worship. Every song made me think of Nathan. Every word made me angry with God. He has violated the trust I placed in Him. I begged Him to keep Nathan and Jenny safe - to watch over them and to protect them. He did not. He did nothing. He let them die a horrible, tragic death. He has broken His word to me. He has betrayed me and my faith is tattered and torn.

My pain knows no bounds. I have spent the entire night in tears. It is now 1:30 a.m. I ache for Nathan. I miss him desperately. I cannot bear this wrenching pain in my heart; every part of my body is tortured. I want to sleep and to never wake up again. I am weary to the bone and so very tired of going through the mechanics of living. I feel more dead than alive.

***

In July of '94 our dear friends, Tom and Linda, lost their youngest daughter Trudi when she was murdered by a convict out on parole. Trudi was two years older than Nathan. They had bonded almost immediately upon meeting each other as very small children; they went to the same grade school and high school together; she called him her "little bro" and he referred to her as his "big sis."

In a small, rural community such as ours, it's not uncommon for everyone's kids to belong to everybody else in that we each look out for the other's. But as is the case universally, there are always those few who become integrated into your family, who invest themselves and their love into your lives, who call you Mom and Dad and think of your home as their home away from home. Such was the case with Trudi.

When we got the news in the wee hours of the morning that Trudi had been shot, I genuinely felt as if I had lost my oldest daughter. I couldn't believe the incredible pain I felt, not just for myself and my own loss, but for Nathan who was absolutely beside himself with grief, and for Linda and Tom whose baby girl had been taken from them.

Because of my deep love for Trudi, I thought I could understand what Linda must be feeling as a mother who has lost a child. Consequently, I made a few of the more classic faux pas in an attempt to comfort her. I had always prided myself on my ability to make honest and accurate assessments of any given situation, even tragic ones. So, from my mouth fell what I thought certain she would need to hear - that we could be certain Trudi, a committed Christian, was with God; that we could take some relief in the fact that her death was quick; that we could hold on to the great hope of seeing her once again in heaven; that God would undoubtedly use this tragedy and bring good from it.

It wasn't until we lost Nathan that I realized that I had not even a clue as to what Linda was feeling, nor could I have, and that <u>nothing</u> I could have said at that point would bring any comfort. Though I loved Trudi as my own, it was not my flesh which had been ripped from me by death; it was not a part of my heartbeat which had been silenced forever; it was not part of my spirit and soul which forever would be lost to me. And the last thing any parent wants to hear immediately after losing a child is that his/her child's death will bring about a greater good. The agony of one's soul in the early stages of grief does not allow for any sense of goodness in death.

After Nathan's and Jen's deaths, equally well-intentioned friends and loved ones would make the same overtures to me. At that point, I did not care that they were in heaven - I wanted them here with me; I did not care that I would see them someday in the "sweet bye and bye" - I wanted to see them now; I did not care that they had not suffered but instead died upon impact - I didn't want them dead at all; and how in the world could any good come from such a tragedy as this?

My friends and loved ones were equally as clueless as I had been, for there are no words to explain or make another understand the profound depth of the pain in losing a child. There are _no_ words to make it better.

***

Nov. 25, 1994

Linda and I have returned from Appleton. Seeing Trudi's murderer at his arraignment has reactivated all of the initial feelings of anger, denial and pain I first felt when Nathan called me at 2 a.m. to tell me that Trudi had been shot to death. It has also rekindled my doubt about God's omniscience and sovereign goodness.

Three of my children gone in three months' time. What mother can endure such heartache? Just when I feel as if I have taken a small, courageous step forward in this process, some seemingly insignificant event slaps me backward two giant steps.

I still do not sleep well at night. My stomach continues to give me a lot of trouble. My concentration level is minimal at best. I can't imagine finishing out this semester except for the graciousness of my professors in allowing me take-home tests rather than comprehensive, objective ones.

I can't remember what it feels like to _not_ be in pain; to sleep and wake up refreshed; to laugh and feel release.

I want my life back and yet intuitively I know it will never happen. I am irrevocably altered emotionally and psychologically, perhaps even spiritually. My life will never be the same.

Dec. 4, 1994

Mike and the girls went for a tree this morning. They have wanted to put it up since Thanksgiving. I am not discouraging it only because it seems important to them. I dread seeing it up - ornaments that are Nathan's - traditions now altered - holiday celebrating that is no celebration at all, just empty, mocking symbols of loss to me. But the girls have had their own loss and I cannot deny them this, too. I can't imagine how I will get through this season.

I went to church while they tree hunted. I barely survived worship and ended up leaving half-way through the teaching. I can't seem to sit still for very long and I still can't concentrate on anything for any length of time either.

My mind wanders and, when it settles, it is focused only on questions which seemingly have no answers, and the ever-present, all consuming "Why?"

The greatest challenge to my faith comes not with questioning if there is a God, but if He is, in reality, who I had always believed (or at least supposed) Him to be. Where is the compassion for my pain? Where is the healing for my brokenness? Where is the guidance for this journey into the unknown of grief? Where are His arms when I ache for comfort at 2:00 in the morning? And most important, where was He when my children needed Him most?

Will I ever be able to trust Him again? Will my love for Him always be tempered with fear and suspicion of His intentions toward me and those I love? I wonder.

Dec. 7, 1994

I have had a terrible day at school, but I don't know what triggered it. I think that when I purchased a piece of artwork with money the University had given us to memorialize Nate and Jen, it must have set new pain into motion. The artwork itself is incredibly beautiful - two eagles soaring over a mountaintop. A plaque at the top is inscribed with a paraphrased verse of Scripture from the book of Isaiah: "Those who trust in the Lord will soar with wings like eagles." It speaks volumes of who the kids were and the importance of their faith to each of them.

How tragic that such a beautiful piece is to memorialize the death of my son and his wife rather than to celebrate their lives. It only reminds me anew of how very much I've lost, and the pain of that recognition is unbearable.

How I long for him - his voice, his touch, to hear him play the piano and sing silly songs for Sarah, to hear the bounce of a basketball on the driveway and the giggle of Rachel as he shoves her around under the hoop. Vast portions of our lives have been ripped from us. How does one live with such vital parts missing and irreplaceable?

Dec. 9, 1994

Terry and I are meeting at Peking Restaurant for lunch. What an immense blessing she has been to me during this time especially. I have grown to love her deeply. I think she will be an incredible social worker. I always find myself feeling at least a small sense of anticipation on Fridays because I know I'll see her.

She offers me herself, and an environment which allows me to be real, whether happy, sad, intellectual, or as in recent weeks, hurting and miserable. Her very willingness to be with me, even in these conditions, is therapy to me. I need to tell her that the next time we're together. She is a sister, a friend, a gift.

Dec. 10, 1994

I am so disoriented today and quite sad...no tears, just a sense of genuine lostness. I cannot task. My focus is fragmented and disorganized. I feel really tired - not sleepy, but physically drained, almost like coming down with the flu.

Dec. 11, 1994

It is 6:30 a.m. I have awakened from a horrible nightmare. I dreamed I drove by the cemetery and I saw Nathan walking among the headstones. I stopped the car and ran to the fence. The gate was still locked. I screamed out his name to get his attention. He turned casually, said, "Hi, Mom" and kept walking. I begged him to come open the gate. He seemed not to hear. I yelled for him to come to the fence and be with me and he turned, gave me his goofy grin and said, "I can't. I have to go now. Jenny's calling."

I began to sob and plead for him not to leave, but he disappeared and then I awoke, dripping wet with perspiration, tears streaming down my face, calling his name out loud.

Mike woke up and, upon realizing what was going on, tried to get me to lie back down to rest. I did, but I wept uncontrollably for well over an hour. I don't remember hurting like this since the funeral.

P.M.: I spent all morning in bed, all afternoon on the couch, totally debilitated by grief. I literally came apart "at the seams" as they say, and I could not find the wherewithal to pull myself together. I have never been so uncontrolled or so frightened.

I couldn't understand what was happening to me, and there seemed to be no way to prevent or change it. It's as if my mind and my body simply could not go on and there was no recourse left to me but to unequivocally give myself over to it.

Though I had done absolutely nothing all day, I went to bed early tonight feeling utterly exhausted. The mere recounting of it now is fatiguing. Maybe I am having a breakdown - is this what it means to lose one's mind - to lose touch with reality? Can I have been so damaged by the pain of my loss?

Dec. 12, 1994

A.M.: I don't know what's happening to me. Am I experiencing anniversary grief? It's been two months since their deaths. Today would have been Trudi's twenty-second birthday and now she is gone, too.

I can't go to school. I hurt too much and I can tell I'm right on the "edge." But I must go. It is my last day. I need to pick up tests. I will shower and simply do it.

P.M.: I cried all the way to school - ended up in Katherine's office, where I cried also. I told her that I didn't understand what was happening to me. She assured me it was a "normal" part of the process. (How can this be normal?)

I realize, in part, that I am just beginning to acknowledge the pain I feel at losing Jen. My grief over Nathan has largely overshadowed the impact of losing her also. Maybe that was what these last few days have been about - starting over in the grieving process, only this time for Jen. Or maybe this simply is all part of the grief, whether it's for Nathan or Jenny - the constant, unrelenting pain that prods and pokes.

Katherine shared that she feels God has designed us in such a way so as to experience grief in bits and pieces - that the whole of grief at one time would most likely destroy us. She is probably right on both counts. There are those days when I feel consumed, and just when I feel I can endure no more, it subsides briefly, even passes briefly, and then it begins again. I long for just one day with no pain, no longing, no heartache. I wonder if it will ever come? Can you ever let go of one whom you have loved so deeply and to whom you have been so inextricably linked?

***

Katherine, associate professor of English at the University, and I had been friends for a few years already before Nathan and Jen were killed, but her friendship after their deaths proved to be an invaluable aspect of my sense of well being generally, and specifically contributed to my ability to continue my education at the University rather than on another campus.

Several mornings a week as I would walk into the Library building the first sight that greeted me was a light shining into the hallway from Katherine's office. Occasionally I would stop in to quickly say hello. At other times I would simply head for my own office. But always I would think, "Katherine lost her daughter and she has survived the experience. She is a warm and loving person in spite of her pain. I can do this, too. I can survive. I can continue to be a loving person in spite of my pain."

I knew that someday I would need, and want, to tell Katherine what her "light" had come to mean to me.

* * *

With Christmas and the holidays came a variety of new and more intense feelings about losing the kids, about life and death generally, and a very keen perception that, in reality, little of my life was making sense anymore.

Mike and I seemed to live in extremes. Either we were uncompromisingly sympathetic to one another's pain and difficulties, or we were so remote and disconnected that we seemed to hardly know one another, much less to care to make the effort to comfort.

I began to withdraw even more from the very people who could have, perhaps, offered me some solace. I did not want to be with my church family. Though extremely compassionate in one sense, they also were naively trusting that I was starting to "do better." I felt certain I was disappointing them; consequently, I carried a certain amount of guilt that I was not, in fact, being strong in my faith and moving on with my life.

I didn't want to be with family, friends or people generally, either. Everyone's lives had moved on; their kids were home from college for the holidays; their kids were announcing engagements or pregnancies; they jokingly grumbled about the extra laundry they now had with the arrival of kids and their friends from college and dorm life. And I would sit there thinking what I wouldn't give to be able to grumble about the price of wedding announcements or having to do extra laundry.

No, I didn't want to be with people. I did, however, find myself wanting to write my poetry again, but nothing except blank pages greeted me after hours of intense pondering. I felt sure there were volumes of feelings and words trapped inside me. If only I could find the key to unlocking the first of them, the rest would certainly come tumbling out.

Then it happened quite unexpectedly. I was sitting alone in the living room. Everyone else had gone to bed and I was, as usual, feeling exhausted but unable to sleep. The room was dark with the exception of one string of miniature lights on the Christmas tree which cast a surreal glow across the ceiling. Under different circumstances, I would have delighted in the serenity of the moment and would have found peace in tranquil thoughts of my family, Jesus' birth, and my once-strong and vibrant faith. But nothing eased the torturous heaviness in my breast; there was no courage left in me with which to fight the nagging unanswered questions; I could find no grace to sustain the agony of being separated from one who was my very flesh and blood; I began to write.

Kathi Pollard

A Mourning Passage

Familiar comforts fail me.
Rest evades my overwearied body.
There are no answers to divine enigmas.
The torture of the present overshadows
The grace yet to be revealed,
And courage to claim it escapes me.

I long for the meaning and purpose of their absence,
But grief cloaks the inaudible answers
From heaven's residents.
We were pilgrims together
Wending through unknown country,
Destined for Home.
I always assumed it would be I
Who would grace the threshold of
Eternal glory to welcome their arrival.

Present and future joys of motherhood
Have been stolen from me forever.
Where was He who sees all when
Death was pillaging my life?

In the stillness of the night, I lie
Motionless and wonder if perhaps
Even God doesn't occasionally blink.

When I finished I clutched the notebook to my chest, pulled the afghan over me and slept for a solid five hours, the longest stretch of uninterrupted or undisturbed sleep I had had since Oct. 12. I did not wake up the following morning refreshed, but I did have a sense that, at last, I had taken my first healthy step in this process called grieving. It was both a rewarding and frightening revelation for if, in fact, I was just beginning, when would it end?

Dec. 21, 1994

Judy and I are trying to coordinate a time in which to take the artwork we purchased as a memorial to the children over to the University, but she too is having a very difficult time getting through the holidays.

It is an inexplicable and unique kind of pain to describe to anyone who has not experienced it. I have yet to find an adequately descriptive vocabulary with which to express the enormous void that becomes one's constant companion due to the loss of a child - flesh of my flesh is gone and I am filled with the jagged edges which remain as a result of the part of me which was unexpectedly ripped from my being.

No matter how I move through life, or how delicately I try to work around the damaged area, it pokes and prods my soul - a constant torture to remind me that I am actually alive when I feel so very dead.

* * *

Dec. 23, 1994

I am meeting Judy at UWC to present Dean Schmittke and faculty with the memorial artwork. There is a knot in my stomach and my throat is constricted. I can barely think about doing this - a beautiful piece of work should be a celebration of life not a memorial to the dead.

Every time I look at the two eagles in the picture, I cry. There is something deep at the core of my understanding that finds peace and meaning in the symbolism of eagles soaring above the earth and I am not without a certain aspect of faith with which to embrace the recognition that Nathan's and Jenny's lives have really begun anew, but my mother's heart cannot let go of them from my soul's nest. I do not want them to fly away - not yet, not now, and certainly not this way. And if it must be so, then the deep, unfillable desire of my heart is to take flight with them - to be released from this heartache and my anchor-like body and to soar on wings of eagles.

I have hoped in the Lord, but there is no breeze to lift me to new heights. There is, instead, a gale which dashes my dreams against the ragged edges of reality and which leaves my wings broken and in terrible pain.

Dec. 24, 1994

I awoke this morning with such aching loneliness for Nathan. People try to convince me that once the holidays are over it will get easier. I don't believe that. I think time will teach me how to more effectively cope with this heartache, but it will not remove it, ever.

I saw Jane (the professor with whom Nathan had his very last class the day of his death who had already become a friend of mine) yesterday at Dean Schmittke's party where we presented the artwork. Seeing her made me miss Nathan all the more, since he had a real love/hate attitude toward the Feminist Philosophy class he was taking from her. It challenged him on a variety of levels, sometimes creating discomfort to his male sensibilities. But he was so obviously willing to grow from the experience; it gave me great pleasure to discuss some of the more troubling aspects of it with him.

As much as I miss his physical presence, I am equally lonely for his wonderful mind and his willing and open conversations with me. I feel so robbed. To have spent 20 years nurturing him to become a warm, tender, bright young man in full anticipation of many years of a rich and stimulating relationship with my grown child, only to have him ripped from me at the onset of what would have been a wonderful life together - my God, it is cruel beyond words.

We spent this afternoon with Mike's family. Everyone was trying his/her best to avoid talking about Nate and Jen, I assume to protect our feelings when, in reality, Nate's and Jen's absence was so conspicuous that we were all tripping over the obvious. Mike's family are good, caring, loving people. I know they meant well, but all the good intentions in the world still cannot fill the void I feel in my soul. I long for a place of solitude, a place to retreat into my own pain, to deny the reality of the holidays around me and simply feel the anguish in my heart.

I wonder if we are not, sadly, a society which cannot cope with death and, consequently, which knows very little about true grief. Because of our ignorance, do we deny people the privilege of expressing their pain in time of loss once the "acceptable amount of time" has elapsed? Do we deny them a chance to be real, authentically human as it were? Those, like myself, who choose to defy the boundaries of socially acceptable behavior with regard to grief, and who choose to express humanness may discover realities deep within which could become treasures through life's journey, but it is not without a cost.

But then, life taught me long ago that nothing of value ever comes freely or easily.

Dec. 25, 1994

6:30 a.m.: My heart aches for Nathan beyond measure or expression. I am sitting in the stillness of early morning by the tree. We did not put his ornaments on it this year. Perhaps we never will again. I gave Jane his angel and Jen's family his fish. The others lie in the darkness of a box as does his body.

Such holes his death has left in our lives! Who will read the birth story this morning? Who will make silly jokes while we're opening presents, or who will play Christmas caroles on the piano while I fuss in the kitchen?

There have been a few, select moments when I have quietly resigned myself to his absence, but not today. I want him back - to feel his scratchy beard against my face - to hear his music echoing through the house - to watch him with his dad, sisters and wife.

I cannot celebrate the giving of a Son. Mine has been taken away. Angels may be rejoicing, but today it falls on deaf ears.

10:15 p.m.: It is a curious thing - I have very little sense of my own spirituality these days. And what little does exist is perhaps more by rote than by deliberation. C.S. Lewis, in <u>A Grief Observed</u>, comments on the place of religion in his life after his wife's death. He speaks of his willingness to listen gladly to the truth of religion, and submissively to the duties of religion. But, he also acknowledges that if you speak to him of the consolation of religion, he will suspect you do not understand - and so will I.

Christmas of all days has been, until now, a deeply spiritual day for me. I have spent many years tailoring our family's traditions so as to encourage and deepen our faith. Perhaps it is that very faith which now undergirds what small shred of sanity I still possess, but there is little if any consolation in my belief of a hereafter so overwhelmed am I with my present pain. It overshadows all else. And while I have never embraced God with the sole intention of planning to avoid hell as opposed to an assurance of heaven, it is my only focus when I try to rediscover my spirituality now.

That Nathan and Jenny are "safe" in heaven should be a consolation, but I should not have to be in a place where this kind of consolation is necessary in the first place, which then brings me full circle as to the question of my own heart.

Where is God when I need Him most? Is He quietly residing in the darkest and deepest crevices of my soul, waiting for my beckoning? Does He hide Himself from me, like an offended lover who discovers that my love for Him can be tempered by circumstance? Has He withdrawn from me until I can admit to Him, and even more so to myself, how very conditional my love has been? And if so, has He not reasoned with Himself that I am, after all, merely mortal, merely human, a creation and not the Creator? Are not those considerations as He sees me struggle through the mire of doubt and confusion which are now my constant companions?

He cannot expect me to unabashedly embrace Him when mortal thought, at least, dictates a harsh truth - that He violated my trust in Him. And now my always-cautious nature is more than hesitant to abandon myself again to One who stood by, as if impotent, while life played out its cruel plot.

I am justified in my doubts and until, or unless, He intervenes with some revelation as to the greater truth of this tragedy in my life, I will remain distant. As far as I'm concerned, it's His move.

Now we shall see what kind of God He really is.

Dec. 26, 1994

I am still so very tired constantly, yet I seem to have an enormous amount of nervous energy. I cleaned cupboards and closets today, not because they needed it as much as I needed to keep busy. The girls are struggling with Nathan's absence a lot these last few days. We seem to get through it with productive work and occasional conversations about future family plans, but the conversations are minimal at best and rather stilted. How do you talk about family when part of it is gone? How do you talk about future when the pain of the present overshadows all else, including a desire for any more tomorrows?

Dec. 27, 1994

Rachel is far too collected yet, and I worry. She doesn't alter her schedule at all to accommodate what I suspect is a seething torrent of emotion just under the surface. She eats and sleeps and laughs with her friends as if there's absolutely nothing wrong with her.

More upsetting is the fact that she is developing a series of very dependent relationships with young men at school with whom she has nothing in common - but, alas, they have altogether too much in common with each other. They are all seniors, fair-haired, and far too quick to offer her "consolation" in her loss of a big brother. It becomes more and more obvious that she is unconsciously trying to replace Nathan in some way. She cannot, of course, see it; neither can they. I have spoken with her about the possibility of seeing a counselor, either alone or together with me or her Dad, but she refuses, always with the explanation that she's "just fine."

Denial in the first stages of the grieving process is almost an imperative to the maintenance of one's sanity. It buffers one from the psychological trauma of an unexpected, and in our case, untimely and violent death of a loved one(s). But Rachel's denial is lasting too long; she is <u>not</u> fine; something has to give; I'm frightened for her.

Dec. 28, 1994

We have found that Rachel has not been honest with us about her whereabouts and with whom she is socializing. Her girlfriends are covering for her so that she can spend time with a young man, one of Nathan's friends. He is already graduated from high school; she is but an eighth grader.

I spoke with Rachel, trying to gently suggest that he is not really the one in whom she is interested; rather, he is serving as a replacement for Nathan. She became very angry, more angry than I've ever seen her before, and I was to some extent actually relieved to see the anger. At least it was a genuine emotion which she was expressing. We have given her no alternative now. She <u>will</u> see a grief counselor; we will make the arrangements and have offered to go with her. She refuses to have us be a part of the process, but has finally agreed, reluctantly, to go. Perhaps her counselor will be able to reach her; we have not been able to do more than offer her abundant love and support which, while immensely important, has not been the catalyst for her to release the pain she has locked inside her.

I ache for her, especially when I see her move into one of her "brave" facades. I cannot know her pain, but I know my own all too well and on most days feel as if I will certainly never recover from it. And if I do, I will be so scarred that I shall never love as deeply or as intensely again for fear of what loss of that love could do to me. I suspect Rachel is feeling the same.

She adored Nathan. He was more than her big brother; he was her hero, her basketball mentor, her friend and companion. Jenny had become the best big sister any younger sister could have asked for and Rachel, who does not give her heart easily, gave hers over to Jenny without hesitation. Suddenly Rachel has been forced to deal with not only the deaths of her two most beloved siblings, but has had to face the whole question of death and her own mortality at such a very tender age.

All of my psychology classes and counseling training has prepared me intellectually to give the right responses and to understand, in theory, what is happening to her, to our whole family, but no amount of education can prepare one for the emotional devastation that the death of a family member wreaks upon one's life. I am quite lost as to know what else to do for Rachel. I feel quite lost as to what to do for myself, for that matter.

We go through the mechanics of living while carrying death inside of us. It is a frightening prospect that this kind of grief will be eternal, in some form or fashion. Yet I cannot imagine not grieving this loss, on some level, for the rest of my life.

* * *

Rachel fell into the classic sibling pattern of behavior - she chose to contain her pain, to not discuss it with us for fear that she would create even more pain for her family by talking about her own suffering. I knew that in her young mind she had rationalized that expressing her pain in losing Nathan would hurt me the more, and she did not want to carry that kind of guilt. Once she began therapy, we saw a bit of the old Rachel start to emerge. And once she was assured by an objective third party therapist that, in fact, it caused us more heartache to watch her holding her pain inside, she began to express some of it with us.

Because she has always been a relatively private person, many of her thoughts were expressed in a journal she began to keep. How proud and pleased I was to watch her begin to chronicle her feelings and to know she had begun the difficult task of mourning the loss of Nathan and Jen.

Once I could see that Rachel was heading in a healthier direction, I began to direct some of my energies to my own ongoing grief work. I knew it was imperative that I continue with my journaling, but I found a renewed desire to get back to my poetry as well. In the process I made an interesting, if not sad, discovery - that I had, in the past, always written out of the abundance of my heart, life and experiences. Now I found myself writing out of the void that existed in my soul. All of my pieces were dark, somber, maudlin, and not a little despairing. That was perhaps good for, while it made for difficult reading, it was, at least and in fact, an honest expression of my existence at that point in time.

I had always been fascinated with the Japanese form of poetry known as Haiku, particularly the more difficult and very structured 5-7-5 syllabication format. On evenings when sleep evaded me, or at times when I had an abundance of nervous energy and had run out of cupboards to clean, I would sit down and try to write Haiku about my feelings.

Haiku

For Nathan & Jenny

Rocking at dawn wrapped
in quilts of longing and grief,
my soul feeling cold.

Hyacinths still bloom
even though my heart lies
buried in fall's leaves.

***

I look for his face
in every blue car I see,
longing for his smile.

Life Cycles

Autumn leaves falling
Two tender spirits ascend
Death transfigures life.

Granite marker set
Above three heads joined in rest.*
Peacefully they lie.

Snowstorm's ragged edge
Embraces fragile spring blooms,
Virgin blush destroyed.

Clamoring children,
Important revelations
Take flight in the din.

Seasons whirling by
Deep-etched grief-filled furrows are
Measure of life's toll.

Enigma revealed
For those of us left behind.
Tears nourish our souls.

*Nathan's and Jenny's stillborn daughter, Angel Marie, was buried at the feet of her maternal great-grandfather. When the children were buried, Angel was exhumed from her resting place and interred between her mother and father.

Jan. 6, 1995

I have struggled since Nathan's death with the deep conviction and subsequent guilt and anguish that I could have prevented the accident from happening had I only listened to what I've always called my "sixth sense."

I felt so very strongly that I should wait for them after class that day, and all the way home I had a very uneasy feeling. Why didn't I listen to those inner promptings? What if they had been delayed by my staying only five minutes - perhaps the truck wouldn't have been on the road they took home - maybe they would have followed me down First Street to their house rather than taking the truck route on Third. Were their lives, and ultimately mine, hinged upon my sense of timing, their sense of timing? Why didn't I respond to the urges and rhythms within me? I did not listen....will it haunt me forever? Can I live with this unforgivable sense of responsibility? Please God, assure me somehow that it was <u>You</u> who called them home, and <u>not</u> a chance circumstance or my own negligence that took them from me!

* * *

I had known other grieving parents who spent years trying to answer the "what if" and negotiate the "if only" of losing a child. When I would listen to their tortured conversations, it was always with the thought that they were unnecessarily punishing themselves for circumstances beyond their control. Inevitably, however, I found myself in the throes of the same pattern for several months.

Intellectually, I could assess the situation, but I could not separate my intellect from my emotions which dictated that as a parent it was both my obligation and privilege to protect my children - to be nurturing while they were yet growing - to be wise while they were yet learning wisdom - to be perceptive of future needs while they were yet living in the reality of the moment.

The untimely death of my children unconsciously forced me to question my ability to care for that which was most precious to me, and no amount of intellectual reasoning could dissipate the invasive thoughts and subsequent heartbreak of "what if?" or "if only." I suspect that, on some level, it will always haunt me. Reason be damned, for all my tortured soul could hear was the destructive whisper of an unanswerable question.

Jan. 7, 1995

What a miserable day. I spent almost the entire morning in tears and the afternoon debilitated by deep agony of separation, triggered by some brochures of headstones which arrived in the mail. One example in particular had Nathan's and Jen's names engraved on the front of the stone, and then on the back was engraved, "Whither thou goest, I will go."

That they "went" together has been a source of deep anguish for me. To have lost both of my precious ones in one fell swoop is more than any parent should have to endure.

And now, to have to choose a stone which marks their graves is too difficult. Sometimes I wonder if I've really accepted that they are dead - my dreams are about them still being alive. I still find myself wandering through the men's department in stores, looking for those "little things" I always would find for Nathan. I can only assume my mind and body are still working through the grief in increments in order to maintain any sense of balance, sanity and health.

Jan. 8, 1995

Dear Nathan,

I have just returned from church, and for the first time since your death, I've made it all the way through without the terrible pain of recognizing yours and Jen's absence during worship.

Remarkably, I actually, for the briefest moment, realized and even appreciated that while I was worshipping God from a distance, you and Jen and Angel were actually worshipping and adoring Him at His throne.

I long to see you just once more. I wish you could send your angel to me to tell me you're happy and at peace. I know it wouldn't be heaven if you could experience anything but joy, so I understand you can't be aware of how desperately I miss you because that kind of knowledge would be painful to you. I feel so selfish for wanting you back when I know you're in the best and most loving place ever. It's just that I long for the connection to be restored - it's so painful to have it gone.

I remember your junior year, when you rebelled so terribly against everything that was, until that point, sacred to you. I would lie in bed so many nights and worry if you were safe, and would pray that you would get back into a committed relationship with God and family. Mostly I would pray that nothing would happen to you because I knew you were not ready to meet the Lord.

And then you did - you turned your life around and began to live out the truths of loving God and family. You married a wonderful girl, took a good job and continued your education. I was so excited to see you growing up, maturing into a beautiful human being, full of love and goodness.

But a part of me had a deep suspicion which I have shared with no one. My one great fear was that you were the kind of man who was easily influenced and swayed by your circumstances and consequently could have allowed yourself to ever-so-slowly slip away from God and us once more.

I Climbed A Mountain

I cannot imagine anything more painful than what I've just been through, to bury you, my precious firstborn, my only son, unless it would be this - that you would have been given a longer life with me here, only to have you turn from God and to not be in a place spiritually to meet Him should you be called to His presence unexpectedly, like now.

It is my only consolation, Nathan, in all this anguish - to know you were ready to see the face of God at the moment you left this earth. In my physicalness, it is small comfort, but when I move outside of myself into things eternal, it brings hope to my soul to know I will see you again. And given the condition of the world in which we live, perhaps it will be sooner than any of us knows.

I long for one of your six-foot-two, pick-me-up-off-the-floor bear hugs. I miss Jen's giggle and her loving embrace. Dad is quite a lost soul on weekends without his hunting and fishing buddy. Rachel acts pretty "tough" about it all (but what else would we expect from her, right?), yet I've heard her crying at night and she's hung your locker poster next to her bed. She sees your face the first thing in the morning and the last thing at night. She refused to view your body at the wake - I know it was because she could not handle not seeing your beautiful face. I think she just wanted to remember you the way you were before the accident.

And then there's the "Peanut." She still has a difficult time understanding why you and Jen are with Jesus and not with her. It's difficult to explain something to a child which I myself still do not comprehend. She cries a lot on Sundays. Her tiny, insulated little world has been turned upside down, and her family structure has changed. I don't know how to make it right for her, so I just hold her and rock her and tell her how much we love her. I try to assure her that you are okay - futile, if not sincere, attempts to relieve her anguished little heart.

And so, Nathan, I just wanted to let you know that today I have had the first glimmer of genuine hope - hope that I will survive losing you. And while I do not anticipate that I will ever feel whole again, since a vital part of my very flesh and being is gone from me, I do think I will survive without it - not well, sometimes, and not without a deep pain as a consequence, but perhaps as time moves on, the pain will not scream so loudly, or demand so much attention and I will find ways to work around it, to recognize its existence and then to move beyond it.

I love you. I long for our reunion, to hug Jenny and to hold my first grandchild...and to worship with you again.

Love,
Mom

My faith was returning to me, but in small bits and pieces, none of which, when put together, made the whole that it once was. Just as my emotionality and physicality were fragmented and disjointed, so too my spirit felt as if it was not really mine. I could not recognize it as being a part of me any longer. The faith which had sustained me through so many of life's events had vanished somehow. And if it had not altogether vanished, then it certainly had found a crevice in the deepest parts of my soul which made discovery of it nearly impossible.

My sorrow overshadowed all else in my life including that which had always been most important to me, my faith. But I knew I wanted it back. Intuitively I knew what I would retrieve would be different than the former expressions of faith I had known. I didn't care. I wanted it back.

Jan. 30, 1995

I have never thought much about a God of sorrows. That is, I've thought how God the Father must have sorrowed at the point in time we know as the Crucifixion and, occasionally and especially during Lent, I have thought about His sorrow as it related to the Lamb eternally slain. But He is, and was, and forevermore shall be,

God. Can God hurt? Certainly not, I assumed, since He is after all, God.

Yet greater theologians than I shall ever imagine myself to be have referred to Him as the Man of Sorrows. And if the man sorrows, certainly the God must sorrow as well. I have had a small lifetime to sorrow for the loss of my only begotten son. God, on the other hand, has had an eternity.

Can that be why His heart eagerly longs for all to become His children? Does He prolong His return because He simply cannot bear that even <u>one</u> should be lost to Him?

That I have lost my son has been the deepest, most agonizing source of sorrow humanness can ever experience. The thought alone of the possibility of losing either of my two remaining children causes more anguish than I know I could ever endure. Yet God faces this reality eternally - that He shall "lose" some - that one who was borne from His creative power shall forevermore be lost to Him. Truly that is the sorrow of all sorrows, and well beyond human comprehension.

I have come to no conclusions about such divine enigmas, with but one small exception. I have always assumed that no man could live if he looked upon the face of God because God's face radiates more glory, splendor, majesty and holiness than can be withstood in our humanness. That is perhaps true. What is truer still, I now believe, is that to look upon the face of God is to behold His sorrow at the loss of His children. To behold that kind of sorrow would devastate and destroy anyone less than God.

Someday, not today, perhaps not tomorrow, but someday I will see the glory in sorrow, for God cannot separate Himself and if He is a God of glory, and if He is a God of sorrow, then they are in some form or fashion one in the same thing. For me, as a Christian then, to embrace suffering is to embrace the glory as well. And to embrace a suffering God is to embrace the glorious God as well.

I have yet to truly know the glorious God for, as yet, I have not known the suffering One. To know the depth of

His anguish will be to know the height of His glory. And who is equal to such an experience? Surely not I, who can scarcely move through a day without languishing and anguishing at my loss. Yet God moves throughout eternity carrying such a burden.

Indeed, He is acquainted with my grief. I am, only now, becoming acquainted with His.

***

February and March came and went. I stayed busy with school work, housework, children's activities, and familial responsibilities. By now the shock and denial were minimal at best; the pain was becoming chronic and constant. There were days when it actually felt good to give myself over to a fit of tears; other days I would pray for the numbness to settle back in so acute was the depth of my anguish.

My professors had been most generous in allowing me to do take-home tests this semester also. I found there were certain times in which I could write. I called them windows of reality - times when my brain actually would function properly and without distraction, but the time frame was limited and the number of times it would happen was infrequent and unpredictable. I found myself sitting at my computer at 2 a.m. to type papers which weren't due for weeks yet because my brain suddenly decided to function for awhile. Then, the following day, feeling hopeful to repeat the exercise, would sit and stare blankly at the screen for hours, barely able to remember what it was I had wanted to accomplish in the first place.

I began to experience a form of chronic forgetfulness. I would get to the store and could not remember what it was I had wanted to purchase. I would go from the living room to the kitchen and, by the time I arrived in the kitchen, had forgotten why I had wanted to be there. I had, prior to the children's deaths, been an extremely methodical, logical, analytical and structured kind of person. Now I couldn't remember important, much less insignificant, details about my life; I couldn't function sequentially. I would get up in the morning and actually have to remind myself that the first thing I needed to do was to shower, then to eat breakfast, then to, then to, then to. I lived in a constant state of panic, aware that I was forgetting something, but I never could remember what the "something" was.

I understood, intellectually, that the whole of the grieving process required a great deal physically and emotionally. I knew, equally well, that sleep deprivation can do horrendous things to one's mind. But knowing facts and experiencing the realities of those facts are far different from one another. So many nights I would lie in bed and wonder if I wasn't perhaps losing my mind. A part of me hoped it was so. It would be blessed relief from the torture of the thoughts which now resided there.

* * *

At the beginning of March, I began to battle with a series of sinus and bronchial infections. During one of my visits to the doctor's office, I stumbled upon a small brochure which discussed the importance of maintaining a regular regimen of physical exercise while dealing with grief. I was already aware of this fact, but had chosen throughout the course of my grief work to ignore it, for a variety of reasons.

I was more than a bit concerned about the fact that I had lost what, for me, was a substantial amount of weight after Nathan's death. Normally weighing in at about 100 pounds soaking wet, I went down to 91 pounds immediately after the accident and had managed to regain only five pounds in the course of the next four months. It seemed to me that the last thing I wanted to do was to exercise and take a chance that I would subsequently drop additional weight.

Of equal concern to me was the fact that, since my own car accident years ago, my spine and left knee could no longer endure the abuse of running/jogging; even moderate jazzercize programs and light aerobic exercise caused me to limp for several days afterward due to a swollen knee and jarred spine.

However, it was also quite apparent that I needed to do something with the chemical changes I could feel taking place in my body as a result of grief work. On some days I would actually feel nervous and jittery, as if I had had too much caffeine. I usually chose to address the changes by scrubbing floors or tearing apart closets.

But there are only so many floors in my house which need scrubbing, and the closets were still organized from my last frantic episode of cleaning. I knew it was time to re-think my decision about formal exercise and to find a way to routinely help my body release the pent-up energies that were exploding inside me.

After much trial and error, I decided upon a Monday, Wednesday and Friday afternoon schedule of a two-mile walk, followed by some mild weight-lifting to strengthen my upper body. It proved to be one of the best decisions I had made for myself in a very long time. I soon was sleeping better than before; my appetite did not necessarily increase, but it did hold steady so that even on days when I was particularly melancholy I still ate regular-sized meals; I had fewer days of the intense "jitters" I had grown so accustomed to living with prior, and I found that facing the inevitable anniversaries which continued to present themselves month after month was at least a bit less physically draining than before.

By mid-March, I was intensely committed to my exercise program which proved to be an invaluable asset as we moved toward March 23, the day Jenny would have celebrated her 19th birthday. It was no less emotionally demanding a day for any of us, but for me it was the first anniversary in which I was able to maintain some semblance of physical well being while working through the grief which inevitably became more pronounced as I dealt with all of the feelings which accompany another significant event.

I had not made any entries into my journal in the month of February or the first part of March so busy had I become with maintaining an exercise regimen in addition to my school work and family responsibilities, but with Jenny's birthday came a renewed longing to get back to my writing.

March 23, 1995

Dear Jen:

It is your birthday. It is painful to remember, yet my mind is flooded with memories of you - you at the dining table - you folding laundry with me in the living room - you letting me feel Angel "kick" for the first time - your hugs, your laughter, your silliness with Nathan - your love for Sarah and Rachel, Mike and me.

I felt so blessed when Nathan chose you for his wife. I knew I had gained a daughter and a friend. I grew, quickly, to love you and to cherish our relationship.

I cannot bear that you are gone. To have lost Nathan was, and continues to be, too painful to even express in words, but to lose you both has left me deeply, deeply wounded and scarred for life. I still do not sleep well at night. Often I wake up with some perverted sense that this is all a dream somehow - that you're just "gone" for awhile, but certainly you'll return and fill this terrible void inside me with your love and laughter once again.

I cannot look at young couples that I do not see yours and Nathan's faces. I have often picked up some little thing in a department store, thinking it would go well in your kitchen or living room. Then I must put it back, realizing anew that you are gone.

There are so many things about Nathan that I never got to share with you; so much about you that I never got to learn. I feel so robbed and denied. Part of my family has been ripped from me. Nothing seems right anymore - nothing seems really to matter.

I cry over everything - or nothing at all. Music is the worst. I cannot listen to any of my favorite classical pieces without thinking about the piano piece Nate wrote for you for your wedding. It was genuinely an inspiration. His love for you was deep.

There are those who have suggested that it should bring me comfort to know that you "went" together - that you met Jesus together as husband and wife. I find no comfort in it at all. I am relieved, occasionally, when I realize that you both were committed to Christ and are therefore now in His presence, but there is no comfort in anything, including that knowledge. I miss you too much to find comfort in it.

I often wear the cross necklace I made you. I took it from your jewelry box when we cleaned out the house. I will never forget how your eyes lit up when you opened the box and saw it. I still feel your hug, your joy. It was apparent that you loved God and my spirit rejoiced that you and Nathan were united in your love of the Lord and each other. How could I have known that a year later you would both be gone to be with Him. What a cruel irony.

I went to school today, but my heart was with you. I sat in my office and wept, longing to see your face in the window. I never realized how deeply connected you and I were till you were ripped from my being.

A small part of me thinks about you being the mother of my first grandbaby, but it hurts too much to dwell on it for very long. Sometimes when the sky is incredibly blue and the clouds are billowy white, I wonder if you are holding Angel - if you can look down on us - if Angel will know all about me before we meet one another - if I will be able to hold her.

I loved you as my own, dear Jen, and now I pay the price for that love which has been ripped from me. I do not regret my love for you, only that I do not know what to do with it now that it has no form of expression.

Sarah misses you terribly. She often asks me if you can "wake up now." To see her pain, to feel her confusion, only adds to my own. We are all quite lost without you both. Even Mike, who says little, cried this morning. You were very special to him. He always felt you were the right one for Nathan - we both did.

I thought if I wrote to you it would relieve some of my anguish and perhaps then I would be able to sleep, but like so many nights, sleep is not to be found. Though I am exhausted, with homework yet to be done, I can't sleep. I can't work. All I can do is grieve.

I love you,
Mom

***

I had been trying to focus some of my pain into writing poetry again. I had written a few pieces including one for Angel whose first birth/death anniversary would be marked soon. It seemed like only yesterday that Nathan's phone call would alert us to the fact that something was very wrong with the baby. Although to this day I do not remember the conversation, I still hear the pleading in his voice as he asked, "Mom, can you get to the hospital right away?"

Jenny, not quite into her sixth month, had had an appointment that morning with her obstetrician - a standard visit to do ultrasound and weight check. But there would be nothing standard about that visit, or that day. The ultrasound technician could not find a heartbeat. The doctor, upon consultation, could not either, and Jenny was subsequently admitted to the hospital for further testing which would reveal that, indeed, the baby had died in utero.

After 12 hours of grueling labor, the fruit of her pain and anguish would be to deliver a barely one-pound baby girl who, from all indications, had actually expired a day or so before. Jen's mom and I stayed with the kids for the whole ordeal. We tried to find some words of encouragement and comfort, but what do you say to a young couple who are enduring the labor knowing full well that the baby about to be delivered will not be alive, will not be theirs to hold and cuddle, will not be theirs to nurture and love? Nathan cradled Jen's head; I rubbed her back; her mom rubbed her legs - all futile attempts to make it "right" somehow.

I held Angel Marie, my first grandchild, for only a moment. It was too brief and simultaneously all-together too long. The nurses wrapped her in a tiny pink blanket and put a little knit cap upon her petite head and brought her to the kids. They each held her and said goodbye. She was then whisked off to wherever it is that tiny, dead babies are taken in the middle of the night.

Jenny had a D&C the following morning and was released that afternoon. The following day we had a private funeral for Angel Marie; she was buried in the same plot as her maternal great-grandfather. She would later be exhumed and buried at the hips of her mother and father - a whole family buried in one plot marked by one large gravestone.

April 7, 1995

Angel's birth/death anniversary looms in front of me like the cavernous mouth of some mythical monster waiting to devour me alive...one more "anniversary" to get through. There are millions of thoughts and feelings raging inside me, but I cannot find the words with which to express them. When I do find words, the pieces I write are birthed from this hideous pain that seems to gnaw at my soul. Perhaps there is no language with which to define this form of torture known as grief.

I have felt, quite briefly, wondrously alive and maternal when we babysit for Andrew Nathan (born in January to a dear friend who named him in memory of our Nathan). My arms feel "full" of him; my heart quiets down for awhile; I take joy in his smile and coos. But it lasts so briefly and the pain quickly pours back in as if it now owns me and jealously guards its place in my being. I would yell for it to go away, but unconsciously I understand that it is my connection to Nathan, to Jen. My pain keeps me connected to them. I feel this pain because I can no longer feel them.

April 13, 1995

We have finalized all the details for Nathan's and Jen's headstone. It will be quite beautiful. Their wedding picture will be on the front with the usual information. An etching will be made upon the back of a young couple hand in hand walking a wooded path to heaven. In the sky sits a tiny angel in the clouds with a look of beckoning.

It is perhaps time to do this thing - to pick out a marker - but it feels too soon for me. It makes their deaths take on even more permanency and closure becomes more specific. I have nightmares again of the accident. I had hoped I had passed through this stage, but it returns unexpectedly and throws me off balance for several days at a time. I think I have accepted their deaths at this point in time, but at some primal level the connection is still intact and the letting go of my maternal longing has not yet happened. Maybe it never will. Perhaps that is the torture of a grieving parent - that death does not obliterate the connection, but merely the opportunity to experience it. The connection is eternal and death halts the experience of connecting on a natural level, but the connection continues nonetheless in a spiritual way. And so there is this longing to make that which is spiritual a tangible, natural experience once again. Thus, the torment - the sense of incompleteness, fragmentedness, disconnectedness, that ever haunts my being.

April 19, 1995

I watched, along with the nation, as the news brought footage of the Oklahoma bombing of the Murrah Federal Building with its many offices and, particularly, its Day Care facilities. I could not bear to see the torment on parents' faces as they waited for news of their missing infants and children. That any other parent should have to endure this kind of heartache is torture to my own sensibilities as a grieving mother. This event has left me with more than just cynicism. I feel nothing but dread and hopelessness. What has become of our sense of humanity and brotherhood? Countless lives obliterated with one senseless and inhumane act, all for an ideology which is neither Godly nor even morally acceptable. Why God has not blinked is beyond me.

April 26, 1995

It is a year since Angel's birth/death. Strangely, I am not sad at her passing. In light of all that has since transpired, it was a blessing. But the day itself marks death, and I do not deal well with death itself these days. So, as usual, my longing is for Nathan and now, equally, for Jen. I feel the loss of Jen more acutely than previously, perhaps because the day of Angel's birth was such a powerful bonding experience between Jen and me - a real connection of mother and daughter sharing in the ultimate circle of life - the birth of a grandchild.

There are moments when my mind will traverse dangerous ground. What would Angel have looked like? Would she have been bright and precocious, walked and talked early like Nathan? I do not allow myself to wander too far. It is too painful and it brings me to even more difficult questions. Would he have been a good father? Would he have been a good husband?

That I will never have the opportunity for answers is too painful a reality with which to contend. I feel so robbed and violated. That I intellectually know I will hopefully have future mothering joys with Rachel and her children is less than satisfying right now. I want them with my firstborn. I invested 20 years into Nathan. I gave him the best of me and now the fruit of my love-offering was robbed from me by an untimely death.

There is part of me even now, six months later, that is angry with God. I did my part. I raised him to believe and live out the Biblical truths. Now should have been my crowning glory - time to see the fruit of my faithfulness bear its own fruit. Intellectually, and even spiritually, I know I should be content, perhaps even satisfied, to know he is the ultimate expression of faithfulness by being in God's presence, but the knowledge does not fill the emptiness of my heart or the longing of my soul.

Haiku for Angel Marie

*April 26, 1994+

Dewdrop from heaven
quickly reclaimed; never smelled
of Grandma's perfume.

May 14, 1995
Mother's Day

I seem to measure my life by the coming and going of events and seasons. Every time I survive another holiday or momentous occasion without Nathan and Jen seems like a victory of sorts. It is also a curiosity that the anticipation of a coming event is always equal to and occasionally even worse than the event itself. Today was no exception.

The whole week preceding today has been miserable - so many invading and unexpected thoughts and feelings with which to contend. I am the mother of three, but only two are here to love and to nurture. My own mother, who adored Nathan, is gone now too - both ends of the spectrum are empty of loved ones.

There is a certainty in my heart that Nathan is in a better place which, of course, leaves me feeling selfish for wanting him back. There is little consolation in the realities and joys of what time I did have with him. I want more - 20 years is not enough. I was blessed by his life - I want the blessing to continue. I want to know that others are being blessed by the life I brought into this world, but it will not happen. We have all been denied and I, more than anyone else I suppose, feel the pain of that deprivation. Who am I now? Am I a mother of three? Or of two, and one dead? Will the rip in my soul inevitably force me to mother my girls differently and perhaps less well now that my firstborn is gone?

I worry about clinging too tightly to Rachel or, worse yet, no longer caring to invest myself as completely for fear of becoming so terribly vulnerable in the process. Instead of rejoicing that I have two surviving children, I live with the nagging fear that this could happen again to either or both of them. I feel as if I "hold my breath" psychologically in anticipation of the other shoe to fall, as it were. Every time Rach jumps in a car with one of her friends, I panic inside. If she's even a few minutes late for her curfew, I begin imagining the worst. My mind tortures me and I work conscientiously to try to redirect my thinking, but it's there - it's always there - haunting, poking, nagging, keeping me on the edge. Tears come too easily. Fear never leaves me. Sadness is my constant companion. I wonder if this is part of the first year experience or will I be tortured like this forever?

May 17, 1995

The headstone is now in place over the kids' grave, but I cannot bear to look at it. I don't know why, but I actually feel nauseous just thinking about it.

* * *

May 20, 1995

I cannot get Nathan's and Jen's headstone out of my mind's eye. I thought I would be glad to have it marking their resting place; I thought it would give me some more closure, but instead all I feel is anguish at losing them. It has resurrected some apparently latent feelings with which I thought I had already contended.

I cannot believe what I am feeling - that I abhor the thought of their bodies decaying. I never realized, until this very moment, how very attached I was to Nathan's physicalness. I loved his strong-arm hugs - the way he smelled when my nose would get crunched into his chest while hugging - his large hands and feet - his nimble and eloquent fingers on the piano keys - his grace and strength under the hoop. His very being was flesh of my flesh, and I loved that part of him as much as who he was spiritually, intellectually and emotionally. The headstone marks the place of his decaying. I hate it.

Judy wants to go out this weekend and plant flowers in preparation for Memorial weekend. I will go out of a sense of responsibility and concern for her need to do this, but my heart will be left at home. I will not allow it to take another battering at the gravesite.

Memorial Saturday

Judy and I met at the cemetery this morning. We shoveled up sod, cultivated dirt, planted flowers and perennials, all the while chatting about placement of this flower or that plant, contrast and color. When finally we finished, we both stepped back, stood shoulder to shoulder and surveyed our accomplishments, tears silently welling in both our eyes. Our real accomplishments were not the flowers we had just planted, but the two precious ones buried beneath. We hugged each other in silence - there are, after all, no words.

***

A dear friend, whose son had died of heart complications a few years ago, had informed me about her involvement in a support group for parents who have lost a child. Somehow I could not see myself as being a part of such a group, not because I did not appreciate what they do, but more because I was so caught up in my own pain that I couldn't imagine sharing it with anyone else much less people I didn't know. Conversely, I had been such a terrible "basket case" for so long that I seriously had begun to consider putting myself into therapy, so when she mentioned the meeting to me one Sunday after church, I decided to go.

June 6, 1995
I went to a grieving parents' group tonight for the first time. The couples there were very loving, understanding and supportive. They are each traveling the grief road, as well. But I discovered I am not comfortable with this type of setting - it is far too painful to know so many others are hurting as I do. I am, for now at least, incapable of feeling their grief - I can barely manage my own.

My heart breaks at the thought that so many parents are without a child they loved. To put that much pain in one room is too overwhelming for me right now. It is too emotionally draining and devastating to endure. Perhaps I need more time.

I know that support groups prove to be an invaluable aspect of the healing process for many of those who grieve. It was obvious at the onset that those who were there felt they were being ministered to in their pain. I am glad for them. But, it was also obvious to me that I am not built to respond well in such settings. I'm glad these people have found something upon which to rely while going through the bereavement process. It seems that for me the hope of restoration and healing will most likely come with the deep, long-term, intimate friendships in my life which offer me what I need when I need and ask for it while still allowing me my solitude and reclusiveness when that is important to my own grieving process. Perhaps I will go again at a later date.

June 11, 1995
Dear Nathan and Jenny:
I cannot believe a year has passed since your wedding. On some level, which I have yet to identify, it feels like forever. Your untimely departure from this earth has left such a void in all of our lives accompanied by pain such as I

have never known before and pray never to know again. That I will mourn my loss forever is an absolute certainty in both my mind and my heart. I have yet to pass through a single day without feeling your absence. Some days it is more intense than others, but it is always there.

There are so many things that remind me of you. I suppose that's what makes this pain so constant, so undeniable, so life altering. I sometimes feel like a piece of radar - I pick up every word, action and detail of life around me which is in any way reminiscent of you while absolutely missing altogether the realities and actualities of what's really going on around me. It is a curious thing.

I have yet to play any of my classic/concert music because the piano reminds me of you even though I have had some of my collection since before you were born. It doesn't seem to matter - my mind cannot and will not make the distinction. Every young couple holding hands is you; every motorcycle is yours; every wedding announcement which arrives in the mail is yours; the list of where you "are" yet is endless.

I am working on the antique dining chairs I promised you, but it is the saddest task to perform. They belong in your dining room, not mine. I specifically saved them last year as this summer's project knowing it would be something you, Jen, and I could work on together. I thought we could use that time to continue to discover each other - a bonding experience with my daughter-in-law.

I have not watched the video of your wedding yet. There are some days when I cannot even look at the pictures I have of you on the wall and mantle, and other times when I'm drawn to them several times in just one afternoon. I never know "where I'm at" till I'm actually there - so little certainty and predictability.

Sarah is having an extremely difficult time right now. It's been too long since you've been gone, and she's feeling quite abandoned by you. Her tiny world of six loved ones has been reduced to four, and she doesn't understand why you won't come home to see her. It breaks my heart to hear her cry and to see her pain. I don't know what to do for her, or how to make her understand that you did not willingly or consciously leave her. She thinks you did and it tortures her. I am angry that God doesn't do something for her. She is an innocent and deserves His intervention and comfort, or at the very least, to have her memory altered so as not to be tortured any longer.

Life continues its rapid pace forward and events continue to unfold all around me, but even when I am part of them, I feel as if I'm only on the periphery of it all. I simply cannot enter in fully. It's as if you took some of my most vital parts with you and I have "less" of me with which to do things. To be what I once was is no longer possible, but I am so uncertain as to who or what I am now.

I could not go to church this morning. It was my turn to lead worship. I had to call Kathy and ask her to fill in for me. I knew I could not stand on the platform, look out on the crowd, and not see you in it.

I know you are in a perfect place. Occasionally, I am glad for you, but not today. I want you back in my life, back in my kitchen, back in my arms. I miss you more than words could ever express. I ache for your presence. Perhaps I always will.

I love you, love you, love you,
Mom

June 18, 1995
Father's Day

Dear Nate:

Today was so difficult. Your Dad did not even get out of bed till before lunch. The girls tried hard to make it special. Dad tried equally hard to respond appropriately, but we all "knew." To lose any of our children would be hell, but I think Dad has to deal with the additional loss that you were his only son. His loss is different than mine - he feels it differently for different reasons. But understanding that does not make watching him in pain any easier. We keep going through all these "firsts" and yet I cannot help but wonder how second or third or twentieth anniversaries will be any different. You are gone, and no amount of time can make that right.

Love,
Mom

***

We seemed to move through summer at a turtle's pace. I did not fuss over my flower beds as in summers past. I did not spontaneously plan a little two or three day road trip for the girls and me. I did not read my usual two or three books a month.

On some mornings I would lie in bed, unable to think about embracing the day. Other mornings I would be up, quite literally, at the crack of dawn with no particular objective in mind but to simply be up and doing something with the intense nervous energy which seemed to invade my body without any warning.

It seemed that every month since Nathan's and Jen's deaths had some event in it which was significant either to the kids, or to our family, or to life generally. With the coming of each of those events I would find myself slipping into deeply depressive days and long, tearful nights. Knowing an event was coming did not make me feel prepared; instead the actualities of life gnawed at my soul; I was torn into a thousand pieces with each realization that I would have to endure yet another celebration that would be no celebration at all without my children to be a part of it with me.

July 4, 1995

Dear Nathan:

I took the girls to the parade this morning. The school band went by and I actually looked for you. That there was no tuba player this year seemed only right and fitting. We decided not to stay for any of the festivities which followed. Rachel did not want to be there any more than I did, and Sarah kept asking when you and Jen were going to arrive. She seems to remember every family moment we had with you and now she struggles to make sense of those memories. So do I.

Memories should be such wonderful, comforting experiences. They are, for me, terribly painful and they make the longing so much greater. I ache for you all the time. It never abates. Sometimes the intensity of it reduces me to tearful moments - tearful days. Most times it's a constant melancholy which haunts my being.

I miss your touch, your big hand rubbing my back, the smell of you, the sound of you, your piano playing, our duets, practicing for church with you, your dumb jokes, your introspective questions, your challenging commentary. I miss everything about you. I would gladly deal with all of the difficulties you brought with you through adolescence all over again if I could just have you back - if I could just feel the connection again - to feel anything again but this heartache.

Several people have told me that because we've shared so much that, eventually, all of the "yous" which I so intensely miss will bring comfort and joy with time. I hope they're right - I cannot imagine a lifetime without you with only this heartbreak to connect us.

I love you,
Mom

***

Every so often I would get a burst of creative energy and had learned to "grab" those moments. I had pads and pencils lying all around the house, easily within reach of wherever I found myself at the moment a window of opportunity would present itself. It was at those moments that I was best able to write. Sometimes it was a few lines of a poem; often it was just a thought that would come out so clearly and expressively that I couldn't afford to lose it. Eventually, lines and thoughts became poetry and essays. Occasionally, it actually felt as if my mind was starting to work well again. I found a bit of hope in that thought alone and began to develop a specific journal into which I would enter just my poetry.

***

Innocence Lost

In childlike wonder, I boldly stroked
the clarity of my idealism in watercolor
with the fervor and tenacity of a Michelangelo.

My Mediterranean-blue skyline
always bordered a Kentucky bluegrass lawn,
and the blaze orange sun held a
permanent place in my firmament
picture after picture.

My once soft, supple brushes
sit in their jar, idle now,
crusted and brittle from neglect.

My strokes have lost
innocence and purpose.

My colors have become muted
variations of original hues.

And my once immovable sun
now dribbles jaundiced rivulets
through a hazy winter-gray sky
into parched, mud-brown wasteland.

* * *

Kathi Pollard

Like a stone in my shoe

My grief over losing you
Is like a sharp, jagged stone
Lodged in the insole of my shoe.

It rips a hole in my stocking,
And pierces my tender skin.
Midnight blue bruises settle in.

Whether I trod courageously forward,
Or despairingly fall two steps behind,
To its permanency I am now resigned.

Perhaps with time my grief over you
Will be a well-worn stone
Embedded in the soul of my shoe.

Time may shift its position,
Or change the meaning of its stay,
But I suspect, alas, it will never go away.

* * *

If I Could Rebirth You

If I could rebirth you with the tears of my soul
And the desperation of my heart, I suppose
I would dress you in navy blue sailor's suits
And read you every Dr. Seuss book ever written.

I would save a lock from your first haircut,
Memorize your toothless chocolate grins,
And bury my nose in the sweetness of your neck
As I tucked you in after your evening bath.

I would courageously walk you
To your first day of kindergarten class and
Never let you see the tears that fell
As I left such a little boy in such a huge world.

I would hold my breath when the training wheels came off,
Help you catch bugs for your first science project,
Cheer the loudest at all your basketball games and
Cook each and every smelly fish you caught.

I would burst with pride and cry at your graduation,
Remind you constantly of my love for and delight in you,
Fall in love with the woman you chose to marry,
And tremble with awe at the birth of your first child.

If I could rebirth you from the joys of my heart
And the pleasure of my memories,
I would do it all the same,
And regret only that you were taken too soon.

***

    I found with my writing a certain catharsis for my pain. The pain itself never abated, but expressing it in some creative thought did ease it, occasionally.
    Summer was winding down which meant, of course, that the fall and school were looming on the horizon. I

was not looking forward to either. I don't think any of us were as was evidenced by the lack of energy and enthusiasm being displayed by each of us throughout August.

Aug. 12, 1995

It's been an unusual and peculiar summer for us all. We move from manic to depressive states, none of us in sync with the others. There are days when I almost furtively devote every ounce of energy to my flowers and the garden only to suddenly find myself in a stretch where simply getting out of bed is a formidable task.

Rachel goes on cleaning frenzies, scrubbing the bathroom, rearranging her drawers and closets for the zillionth time, and then, without warning, she will lie nearly immobile on the couch just staring at the ceiling.

Sarah sleeps a lot these days. She goes to bed early in the evening and awakens mid-morning, groggy and unrefreshed. She asks continually yet when the kids are coming home to visit her. Somehow I have yet to manage an adequate explanation of death which would enable her to understand what "never" means.

We took our annual school shopping trip to Appleton, and did the usual things, but poor Rachel just couldn't decide on anything - so very atypical for her. We did manage to eventually get the basic school necessities - jeans, shirts, and basketball shoes - but it was obvious she felt as I do also - that nothing really matters. Most of life's circumstances are quite superfluous. Compared with the enormity of losing a loved one, all of life's succeeding events are a mere footnote by comparison.

I do not look forward to returning to school, although the discipline will be good for me, I suspect. Conversely, the added stress of performance is something I don't feel I need right now.

Linda informs me, having just passed through a full year, that Trudi's death anniversary marked a turning point for her - that she at least doesn't grieve constantly now, but that when the grief does come, it is actually far more acute. But at least it is not daily and chronic. I hope it is so for me as well. My whole body actually aches yet, and I am weary to my very bones.

* * *

With the end of summer came the harsh realization that I would begin another semester of study at the University and that I would not see Nathan and Jenny there. I spent several days prior to the actual first day of school talking myself into continuing my education at all, much less on that campus.

The whirlwind of activities which accompanies acclimating oneself to a new schedule, new routine, new professors and new demands actually proved to be beneficial in some respects and equally stressful in other ways.

Having our household function on a more specific routine than we had been experiencing through the summer months helped to eliminate the guesswork of what to expect from day to day. Certain activities, obviously, could be anticipated and prepared for. The girls seemed to settle into a routine with little difficulty and after just a few days the household was running rather smoothly. My class schedule permitted me to stay home until the girls got off to school for the morning and allowed me the freedom to arrive home just a few minutes before they did. But it soon became apparent that all was not well.

Shortly after the semester began, Rachel began to complain of headaches and "not feeling good" more days than was typical of any high schooler. Sarah did well the first few weeks and then began to display aggressive and disobedient behavior for her teacher and teacher's aide. Mike admitted to having to do much of his work over again due to an inability to "get it right" the first time through. I found myself, on a number of occasions, actually staring out the window during a lecture in Psychology - usually my favorite subject - because I simply could not attend or focus. I was also becoming forgetful of overlapping demands - when I had scheduled what and with whom. To add insult to injury, we all seemed to repeatedly recycle colds and the flu among ourselves.

It became apparent that each of us was struggling with an inability to focus, attend, and remember, and for each of us, it manifested itself not just psychologically but physically, as well. All I could think about was that it was September which meant, obviously, that October was right around the corner. I filled my personal calendar as well as the family calendar with as much activity as was humanly possible to maintain with the desperate hope that if we expended enough energy and time on activity it would eliminate the amount of time each of our hearts and minds would have to think about the inevitable. Unfortunately, it just doesn't work that way.

Sept. 5, 1995

I went to the string quartet tonight which was performed at the University. Mike's in Wyoming with Dr. John on a well-deserved hunting expedition. Nathan, my usual companion for such events, is gone, and Rachel has little interest in cultural pursuits, much to my disappointment. I found myself sitting alone in an outside aisle seat, and was not necessarily upset by my aloneness, when Jane graciously invited me to come sit with her, Doug, and the Duplers.

While walking around campus during the intermission, all I could think about was Nathan and the many, many events such as this which we had enjoyed together. I especially remembered when we went together to see the Milwaukee Symphony which played in Menominee four years ago. They had performed the week of my birthday. Nathan surprised me with tickets, a corsage and pie and coffee afterward, all of which he paid for with his lawn mowing and paper route money. All I had to do, he said, was "drive us there and look beautiful like you always do. I'll be the envy of every guy there, Mom!" He was 15.

The memory should bring me joy and great pleasure, but for now, it only reminds me of how much I've lost.

I read an article last week in Psychology Today which suggested that for many mothers the second year of grieving the loss of a child is actually far more debilitating than the first. I was glad to have that knowledge since on any number of days I have wondered why, in fact, the pain continues to be even more pronounced rather than to have diminished a bit. It would seem that we mothers have a tendency to put our own grieving on hold to some extent in order to facilitate sound mental health for the rest of our family, which I find is an accurate depiction of my own circumstances. Now that the girls seem to be doing a bit better, I find I have the "leisure" (if one dare to call it that) of more deliberately addressing and working through my own pain.

It is one thing to lose the connection with a child himself, but for mothers, in particular, there is a realization somewhere at the end of the first year that we have lost the connection of "self" as well. I know this to be true for me. It certainly explains this awful uncertainty and chronic melancholy which I am now experiencing and which seems to be superimposed on my grief for losing Nathan and Jen.

I thought perhaps it was due to the anniversary being just a few weeks away. I'm sure that's part of it, but something else is happening to me. I feel as if I have no soul - that somehow I need to recreate myself. I don't have any idea as to how to go about such a task. I don't even know if I want to, or if I have the energy to do so.

All of my writings, especially my poetry, are dark and hopeless with such a lostness about them. And so I begin to see - not only have Nathan and Jen been lost to me, but I am, in some inexplicable way, lost to myself - a seeming shadow of the formerness I once was, and a veritable question mark as to whom I shall become.

***

Every day which passed between September and the anniversary date (Oct. 12) was supreme torture. I would wake from a restless sleep feeling utterly exhausted and the first thought which became a cogent component of my understanding was that I had lived almost a whole year without Nathan.

As I pressed on through each day, every single event in that day seemed to mock me. Every song reminded me; every young couple reminded me; every motorcycle reminded me; every mother holding a little boy reminded me; every young man at gas stations, department stores, church, anywhere, reminded me. It was as if the whole world shouted to me - "Nathan is gone. Nathan is dead. Nathan will never come back to you."

Suppers which, prior to Nathan's death, had been delightful times of catching up with one another, laughing at silly jokes, planning the week's activities, became agonizingly silent experiences with only snippets of conversation between any of us. I think we simply didn't have any energy left by evening since most of it had been spent just getting through the respective demands of each of our day's events.

Bedtime came early in those days, if not because of utter exhaustion, then because it was a form of escape to our own private sanctuaries. But most nights sleep evaded me. I found myself with the same kind of restless, anxiety-filled insomnia as in the first weeks after his death and always with the same conflicting thoughts, either that this really was all a nightmare and it would be over soon, or that this was the worst experience of my life and soon we would mark the first of many anniversaries to come. There was not one night in which my pillow remained dry those nights and I would long for the morning to come so as not to have so much time to think.

Morning would come only to remind me of the necessity of having to face another day in which I would long for the night as a form of escape. By the first week of

October I felt certain I would not survive to see the first anniversary of their deaths and equally certain that, unfortunately, I would.

* * *

It's a Year Now

It's a year now.
    The bedroom which once resounded
    With raucous jubilations of teens
    Has been transformed into a study,
    Though little study ever takes place there.

It's a year now.
    The piano and trombone which
    Regaled the household with their tones
    Beg for someone's touch or breath,
    But their pleas are ignored.

It's a year now.
    The favorite apple tree you climbed in
    And fell in love under
    Droops its heavy arms wearily
    Seeking comfort from its burden.

It's a year now.
    The rosebush you helped me plant
    The summer of your marriage
    Did not bloom its beauty this year,
    And now just weeps its leaves one by one.

It's a year now.
    Somehow it feels like a lifetime,
    And my heart's unsteady rhythm
    Confirms my daily suspicions,
    That nothing will ever be the same.

Kathi Pollard

Oct. 12, 1995
2:30 a.m.: I cannot sleep. My heart is tortured beyond description. There is no denial, shock or numbness left to buffer me from the agony of separation. The price of losing Nathan, whom I have loved so unconditionally and unequivocally, is tasking and demanding beyond possible relief. The joy of that deep and abiding attachment is blurred from my heart's vision, for all I can see is the wrenching of my soul.

That grief and heartache should be my constant companions seems only logical and right somehow given that Nathan was always my joy and delight. It is not that I love my daughters less well or less deeply; it is that I have loved Nathan very well and very deeply. We were mirror images of one another in so many ways and on so many levels. Only he and I could love each other as we did. And that love and commitment brought us through some of life's most difficult times, no worse for the battles because we had one another's souls wrapped securely in the arms of love. Now my arms are empty and no one can fill that spot which was solely his.

I know that the depth of my grief is, in fact, because I have loved so well. That I am capable of such a love is remarkable to me - astounding, actually. I have learned many, many things on this journey called grieving, all of which are important, perhaps even significant. But the greatest lesson has been in the learning, or relearning, not about theories and philosophies, but about myself. I have discovered qualities of myself I did not know I possessed.

I have never thought of myself as either brave or courageous, yet I now know there is a quiet courage which dwells within me, which spurs me on through each of my life's difficult events - divorce, single parenting, death of parents, breast cancer, death of a grandchild and now death of my beloved children. I look back on all of the tragedies in my short life and yet I do not feel my life is tragic.

Perhaps Dostoyevsky was right - that which does not destroy us does indeed strengthen us. I am strong, and it is more than sheer determination which fuels that strength. It is hope; hope that I can grow with every new day; hope that I will leave the day and the people I meet in it better for having been part of me.

I have learned that I have the capacity to love meaningfully and deliberately and to extend myself completely to those not of myself. I could not love or be any more fully committed to Rachel and Sarah had they been borne of my womb. Indeed, sometimes I forget that they were not. And when Jenny came into our lives my heart expanded yet again and she became my child as well.

I always thought that someday I would hold grandchildren on my lap and they would giggle when I told them the story of their mom and dad - high school sweethearts, basketball star and cheerleader, Prom King, National Honor Society students, that their mom always caught more fish than their dad did, and she always managed to get him to clean them. So many stories to tell about my precious children. Yes, I have loved Jen, and loved her well. I am richer for that.

I have learned, most importantly, that Christ walked with me every footstep of this journey, but that pain has a way of blinding one from seeing the whole picture clearly. Throughout the course of this entire year, there has not been one week in which I did not receive a card, letter, phone call, visit, meals, hugs, tears or some other affable response to my pain from the Body in Christ.

They have acknowledged not only their connectedness to me, but their devoted willingness to stand with me in my pain and heartache. <u>They</u> have been His arms around me; their tears have been an expression of not only their own sense of loss, but God's awareness of my pain and loss; their comfort has been a vehicle of His comfort. I am blessed to call them my friends.

I have learned that, beyond all else, I am a survivor - that I possess an indomitable spirit which even death cannot destroy - hamper, perhaps, but not destroy.

And, I have learned that I am willing still to continue to love and to be loved and connected, that as trite as the saying is, it is nonetheless the epitome of truth for me. It <u>is</u> better to have loved. My time with Nathan was far too brief, but oh how very rich and blessed a time it was. He, like no one else, helped (and sometimes forced) me to discover and uncover the best parts of me. He took my rigid, disciplined and structured life and taught it spontaneity; he forced me to laugh at myself and to let go of my always-so-serious-let's-be-analytical side; he brought young men and women into our lives who still call me Mom and who, when they return to Stephenson for holidays, insist on a supper "with the family;" he lived life so fully and freely in his 20 years, easily enjoying each moment; he gave me a wonderful daughter-in-law and assured me I was a great mom to them both.

He loved me - with all that he was and all that he had, he loved me. And in his love I found a contentment, a delight, and joy beyond description. That my life will never be the same because of his life is reality. That I shall never be the same because of his death is reality also. If I could have foreseen how briefly he would be with me, I now believe I would have fully embraced the opportunity to still have him only those 20 years rather than not at all. My deep anguish at losing him is a tribute to our love for one another.

His legacy to me is to know with absolute certainty that I have been loved. I can only hope that I leave as enduring a legacy upon my own departure to those whom I have endeavored to love.

* * *

I spent the entire morning of Oct. 12 doing several things I had not been brave enough to do throughout the course of the prior months. I read the over 400 sympathy cards and letters which we had stored in a large box in the basement. So many of them were eloquent tributes to

Nathan and Jen. Several were personal testimonies to the love and joy he had brought into others' lives. A few people actually wrote thank-you letters to us for having raised a warm, loving, giving young man whose life was a model for the younger boys at school and within the community. I cried through every one, clutched several of them to my breast when I would finish reading them, and then lovingly packed them back in the box, taped it shut, and put it on a shelf in the closet.

Next I went to my desk and retrieved a video which I had hidden away behind some books. It was a tape of Nathan's and Jen's wedding which I had not yet seen. I wasn't necessarily wanting to relive their wedding as much as I was needing to see their faces again, to hear their voices once more, to feel connected in some small way to each of them again. About halfway through, the photographer zoomed in and there, in living color, was my dear boy's face. I pushed the pause button and sat with my face against the screen of the TV. What I wouldn't have given to feel the growth of his beard on my cheek!

I could watch no more. I wept uncontrollably, but they were not angry, bitter tears. Instead, they were cleansing. I could feel my soul being washed. It sounds so mystical, but it is, in reality, the simple truth. It was as if the pain was lifting me above myself and beyond who I had become in the last year. For the first time since Nathan's demise, I felt that the pain would not destroy me but would, in fact, recreate me somehow. I went to the bathroom and showered and then dressed in my favorite outfit. I wanted to go to the cemetery.

I stopped at the florist and purchased two large bouquets of flowers, each bound by the same teal-colored ribbons Jenny had chosen for the wedding bouquets. It's only a 15-minute drive to the cemetery from our home, but it seemed like it took me an eternity to get there.

As I arrived, I could see Margie the caretaker fussing over a newly dug grave not far from where Nathan and Jen were buried. When she saw me heading toward the grave, she graciously left the area to allow me to be alone with my kids and my thoughts.

It was as incredibly beautiful Indian Summer day as a year ago when the kids were killed. I placed the bouquets in the vases which are on either side of the gravestone, and then sat down on the newly-mowed grass.

The black marble marker glistened in the brilliant sunlight. Their wedding picture stared back at me - two smiling faces to greet my aching heart. Again, I sobbed uncontrollably, but it was a sweet release and a blessed form of healing. I stayed much longer than I had realized because that night I discovered that the back of my neck was quite sunburned. I remember talking aloud with the kids that day; I don't remember what I said, but I do remember feeling, for the first time, a gentle resignation settle into my being. Yes, they <u>were</u> dead; no, they were <u>never</u> coming back; and yes, I <u>could</u> live without them. More than anything else, I remember feeling a peace. It was not contentment, not happiness, not joy of living, but a quiet kind of peace that allowed me to believe that I would survive this experience.

Oct. 12, 1995
10:30 p.m.

Dear Nathan:

You have been the delight of my heart and the joy of my soul, my dear, precious one. That I shall forever mourn losing you seems a certainty; that I will find comfort in knowing we will see each other again and have an eternity together is my great expectation; that I shall live a more meaningful life until then is my constant challenge.

Alas, Nathan, I feel I might be able to begin to put one foot in front of the other and to start anew, without your presence, but ever guided by your footsteps which have gone before me.

I will not allow your death to diminish me; rather I will rely on our love, which we so freely shared with one another, to enrich me and to force me forward. I will try to remember the sound of your laughter when my life becomes sad; I will remember your joy and pleasure in nature when my world becomes dismal or corrupted; and when grief crowds into my soul to lay claim to its terrain, I will stir my soul's memory of your affection and love for me and acknowledge to grief that it is but small price to pay for having had that love for 20 years.

Just recently, I have had these occasional, frail little thoughts about being able to get on with my life. I say "frail little thoughts" because they are merely whispers from my soul - a soul which, since your death, has become something I think you would not even recognize much less appreciate.

I have felt so lost to myself since you died - like the best parts of me were buried with you. The thought of establishing new relationships seemed terrifying to me. Simply being with people was more than I could endure. Even school became a matter of routine and perfunctory response, with many hours spent in the solitude and reclusiveness of my office.

But now, at last, it seems that there may be a bit of a spark returning to my heart. Perhaps this tiny bloom of healing will be nurtured and God will see to it that the right people now come along who will not only love me and nurture health to my crippled soul, but who will also be blessed by my own ability and newly-discovered desire to love in return - people who will draw the love from me until I am healed enough to give it myself without hesitation or compromise.

Alas, my precious one, there is a flicker of hope in me and a small sense of anticipation that while I shall ever be changed for your death, I will rise above the pain to rediscover and, if need be, to recreate myself. I suspect that my grief for you is now becoming manageable. I shall learn to live with this absence in my soul and I shall teach my heart to love again in spite of the huge hole which exists there.

I love you, dear boy. Death may have claimed your body, but I hold you inside me as surely as I bore you in my womb. You are a part of me and nothing, not even death, can ever change that.

I love you, beyond feelings, beyond words, beyond human comprehension.

Always and forever,
Mom

I Climbed A Mountain

I climbed a mountain.
Its jagged terrain clawed at tender skin,
And tortured my unconditioned sinew and muscle.
A ragged peak was bejeweled with flags.
I had not been the first.
I would not be the last.
But, at that moment, it was my mountain,
And I alone had conquered it.

I climbed a mountain
Whose summit held no adulation
From approving crowds and whose
Heights and depths were far more
Vast and profound than I had perceived
Them to be during the journey itself.

I climbed a mountain
Only to discover I shall need to climb another
And yet another in order to make my way across the earth.
I will feel no wreath upon my head but, instead,
God's tender caress upon my cheek and
The warmth of His breath across my soul
Will be reward for the courage it took
To put my feet upon the rock.

EPILOGUE

As of this writing, it has been a little more than two years since my children's deaths and in all fairness to you, my readers, I must confess that in many respects "things" have not changed all that much.

Each of my family members is doing better generally, although we all still struggle to get through birthdays, anniversaries, and holidays. Nathan's and Jenny's deaths have left an obvious hole in our family and in each of our lives which makes even the routines of life, much less traditional celebrations, a difficult experience.

While the commemoration of the first anniversary of their deaths did bring about certain forms of resolution for me as noted in the last of my journal entries, it did not eliminate the gnawing feeling in my gut or the ache in my soul which seem to be perpetual. In truth, I found the second year to be even more difficult to deal with emotionally due to the obvious absence of shock and denial, both of which so eloquently masked what I was genuinely experiencing and which buffered me from feeling anything too intensely or too deeply during the first year of grieving.

Having admitted to my own sense of continued emotional turmoil, I must also honestly acknowledge that, conversely, I am actually doing better in a few ways. I now am able to sleep through the better part of the night; the nightmares which persisted throughout the first year are less frequent and less debilitating when they do occur; my appetite has returned to an almost-normal state and some foods actually taste good to me again; my desire to be with people I care about and my ability to enjoy their company has resurfaced, though it is still far from what it once was; I am now able to talk about Nathan and Jenny and reminisce with friends about shared memories without always falling apart and needing to exit the room; occasional flashbacks and memories of Nathan's and my shared moments will cause a flicker of a smile rather than a deluge of tears; my "bad" days don't last as long and are not quite as intense or debilitating as before.

I cannot imagine that a parent ever fully heals or recovers from the pain and devastation of losing a child. But I do believe that time teaches us how to more appropriately manage the grief and does, in fact, eventually force us to realize our own aliveness and our responsibility to live out our gift of life with as much love and integrity as is humanly possible.

Additionally, I have discovered that as I willingly continue to work through this experience known as grief, I am recreating myself in the process. I have chosen to embrace the philosophy that I will not allow my children's deaths to diminish me for that would give death the final say and the final victory. As a Christian who believes in the resurrection of Christ and all those who believe in Him, I will not allow death to have that kind of power over me.

Instead, I will ask God to use the anguish of this experience to create in me a deeper compassion for those around me who suffer; I will allow God to show me the higher purpose of this experience so that my children's lives will be honored and mine will not be wasted on the futility of self-pity but, instead, will be spent gratefully embracing that which is right, good, and holy about life; I shall live with the hope and faith that tomorrow brings with it a newness which will enrich me; I shall purposefully live my life in such a way that my children's lives live on in me until such time as I, too, am called home to be with my Lord.

I choose to believe that God's grace is sufficient for each new day, no matter what that day holds. I believe God will continue to impart to me His wisdom and that my insight into the matters of life and love will continue to be deepened by my own suffering love. My commitment to that which is important in life is intensified by the realization that life is fragile and uncertain, and never to be taken for granted.

My faith compels me to embrace the reality that it is only through death that one can experience resurrection power. My dear children will be resurrected "on that great and glorious day," and I will, meanwhile, allow God to ever-so-slowly and gently resurrect my weary soul to a newness of life which will sustain me through my days on this earth.

Yes, I am marked by death, but I shall display the emblem as one who, having gone to battle, returns home the victorious conqueror.

> "...that everyone who looks to
> the Son and believes in him
> shall have eternal life, and
> I will raise him up at the last day."

To order additional copies of **I Climbed A Mountain**, complete the information below.

Ship to: (please print)

Name _____

Address _____

City, State, Zip _____

Day phone _____

____ copies of *I Climbed A Mountain* @ $7.50 each $ _____

Postage and handling @ $1.50 per book $ _____

Total amount enclosed $ _____

Make checks payable to *Kathi Pollard*

Send to: **Kathi Pollard**
P.O. Box 105 • Stephenson, MI 49887

To order additional copies of **I Climbed A Mountain**, complete the information below.

Ship to: (please print)

Name _____

Address _____

City, State, Zip _____

Day phone _____

____ copies of *I Climbed A Mountain* @ $7.50 each $ _____

Postage and handling @ $1.50 per book $ _____

Total amount enclosed $ _____

Make checks payable to *Kathi Pollard*

Send to: **Kathi Pollard**
P.O. Box 105 • Stephenson, MI 49887